C A B I N S   I N   T H E   L A U R E L

A CHAPEL HILL BOOK

CABINS IN THE LAUREL

Muriel Earley Sheppard

PHOTOGRAPHS BY BAYARD WOOTTEN

FOREWORD BY JOHN EHLE

The University of North Carolina Press

Chapel Hill & London

© 1935, 1991
The University of North Carolina Press
Foreword © 1991
The University of North Carolina Press

Library of Congress
Cataloging-in-Publication Data
Sheppard, Muriel Earley.
Cabins in the laurel /
by Muriel Earley Sheppard :
with illustrations by Bayard Wootten.
p.   cm.
"Chapel Hill books."
Originally published: 1935.
ISBN 0-8078-1986-7 (cloth : alk. paper).
ISBN 0-8078-4328-8 (pbk. : alk. paper)
1. Mountain whites (Southern States)
2. Blue Ridge Mountains—Social life
and customs.   3. North Toe River Valley
(N.C.)—Social life and customs.
4. Folklore—Blue Ridge Mountains.
5. Folklore—North Carolina—
North Toe River Valley.   I. Title.
F210.S49   1991   91-2943
975—dc20   CIP

The paper in this book meets the
guidelines for permanence and durability
of the Committee on Production Guidelines
for Book Longevity of the Council
on Library Resources.

Manufactured in the
United States of America
95 94 93 92 91
5   4   3   2   1

TO

MARK SHEPPARD

AND

MARK EARLEY SHEPPARD

CONTENTS

FOREWORD

by John Ehle

I'm told that late in life the Sheppards moved to Kentucky where Muriel Sheppard, the author of this book, announced her intention to write a similar book about the people of that region, whereupon she was ordered away at gunpoint. The story cannot be entirely true; Kentucky men are unlikely to draw weapons on a woman, even a writer, but I tell the story because it shows the animosity generated among the people about whom she wrote, a phenomenon not unlike that occasioned by the publication of *Look Homeward, Angel*, about Asheville natives forty miles to the south.

This book is Muriel Sheppard's picture of Appalachians—let each writer have his own—perhaps the best non-fiction portrait we have. Only two other books come to mind as able to hold a candle to it, the two landmark studies by Horace Kephart and John C. Campbell, who also were outlanders, visitors, who saw Appalachians plain.

Mrs. Sheppard arrived with her husband, a mining engineer, and settled in the mining town of Spruce Pine, North Carolina, probably about 1927. She was a shy woman, yet knew her own mind; a friendly person who rarely appeared to feel at ease; she knew nothing about Appalachians but was politely curious, and in time became enamored; she was a poet who could not find audience for her work, or a publisher, either, and doubtless the poems in this book are from her hand.

This was a time of critical transition for Appalachia, and the people tended to separate society into those people who were progressive and those who were old-fashioned. Mrs. Sheppard was thought to be very progressive indeed. Certainly, whenever she and her husband were entertained, she made known what foods and cooking methods she preferred, and what service she was accustomed to, all the latest advice from the best magazines. Also, she wore men's trousers, and if that is not progressive, what is? Also, and this is the crowning proof, she claimed to be writing a book, and that exercise was never before dreamed of, much less undertaken, by any man or woman in Mitchell County.

Later, she announced in her shy way that her book was to be published, and by a university press. Mrs. Bayard Wootten arrived from Chapel Hill to take pictures for it, and she and Mrs. Sheppard together traveled into the coves, seeking evidence of historic lore, old-fashioned styles and customs, stories told in families, most any and every evidence of wear. They sent mountain people back into their houses to change into homespun or linsey, should they appear in store-bought clothes. They sent mountain women to find their hand-thrown pots, to replace the store-bought ones in use. Elderly Mrs. Ellis, proud of her new ware, complained to Rufus Morgan about this. "Mrs. Sheppard insists I have no pot in my springhouse that wasn't hand-throwed; there's not a hand-throwed pot left anywhere around this place."

The first mountain person to read a copy of this book must have realized it was not a description by a progressive writer of a progressive people. Mining engineers opened it, expecting to read about mining innovations, of which there were many of national consequence, and instead read about a shootout at a small, local mine. Ministers, the judges and healers of the mountain people, a self-sacrificing group of servants, opened the book expecting to find recorded samples of their heroic rescues and wise counsel, and instead found described a meeting of a holy roller sect in some remote setting. The annual fair in Spruce Pine was a community effort to honor solid work in crafts, animal breeding, cooking, and so on, but in Mrs. Sheppard's account it was a drinking fest and a bout. Virtually every aspect of life was given an old-fashioned turning.

The pictures selected for use in the book appeared to be out of the past as well, mountainside cabins instead of valley houses and barns. The peoples' expressions were wan, lonely, regretful. The men were presented with child-like, shiftless characteristics. Here is a picture of Sam Brown who looks to be down on his luck, a victim of mountain isolation, while in fact he has been to

Paris to study sculpting. And this pretty girl seeking, or so the caption says, to adjust to changing conditions, why that's Helen Twiggs, and the only change in her conditions is that she has just arrived home on vacation from the university.

Hurt. The people had their feelings hurt; their pride, always close to the surface, was cruelly mashed. They had hoped for better. And Mrs. Sheppard was hurt, too. She had composed a sort of poem to the mountain people in which her images of them were presented affectionately. She had sought to create a work of art, Mrs. Wootten abetting. If judged as a work of journalism, then perhaps it would fall awkwardly, was more true of an earlier day, say 1890 or 1900, than this one, but she was not a journalist in the first place.

Fifty-some years passing have made such time differences largely irrelevant. *Cabins in the Laurel* is for us who write novels a treasure we sometimes mine, and for those curious about Appalachians, historically it is the easiest access. Dee Vance, who today drives the bookmobile in Mitchell, Avery, and Yancey Counties, says she can't have enough copies, often is flagged down on the road by a slender lass or gangling fellow and asked straight-out: Do you have that book? The wayfarer means this book, and will take no other. At the hearthfires, near the Buck stoves of the mountain country, Muriel Sheppard's book now is being read. A friend of mine, Judy Hall, recently gave a copy to her mother-in-law, who had never had a copy in her house. She read it and declared it to be a proper book, describing "just the way it used to be up here." With many converts, in many ways, in our own time the book makes its way into the minds and feelings of the people who were its subject. For them, and for those who are not relatives or natives, it offers the most friendly, easily read, vigorous, zestful portrait of Appalachians we have from the past. It is a work of affection, created for us by a shy lady and her photographer who came visiting, and were understandably chastised, and who have stayed to earn our praise.

ACKNOWLEDGMENTS

It is a pleasure to acknowledge the interest and encouragement of Edwin Björkman while this book was in the making; to recognize my indebtedness to Jason Deyton, who generously permitted me to use as a source of historical detail his unpublished manuscript, "The History of the Toe River Valley to 1865"; and to express my gratitude to John McBee for the use of his files of early land grants. I also wish to thank all those mountain friends whose cooperation in collecting material has made this work possible. Mrs. Marjorie N. Bond of The University of North Carolina Press has aided me greatly, by criticism and suggestion, in the preparation of the book for publication. M.E.S.

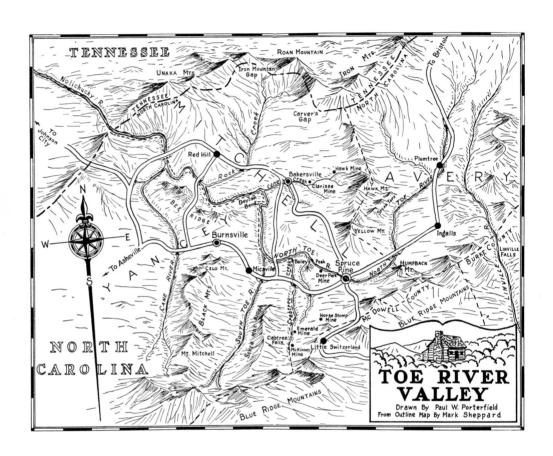

TENNESSEE

Nolichucky R.

Roan Mountain

Unaka Mts

Iron Mountain Gap

Iron Mts

To Bristol

TENNESSEE / NORTH CAROLINA

Carver's Gap

TENNESSEE / NORTH CAROLINA

To Johnson City

Red Hill

Rock Creek

Cane Creek

Bakersville

Hawk Mine

Plumtree

AVERY

Hawk Mt.

Clarissa Mine

Spear Tops

TOE RIVER

BEE RIDGE

Dayton Bend

Burnsville

North Toe

Bailey's Peak

Yellow Mt.

Ingalls

To Asheville

Celo Mt.

Micaville

Spruce Pine

North Toe R.

Humpback Mt.

BURKE COUNTY

LINVILLE FALLS

CANE RIVER

BLACK Mts.

South Toe R.

Toe R.

Crabtree Creek

Deer Park Mine

McDowell County

Blue Ridge Mountains

LINVILLE RIVER

Horse Stomp Mine

NORTH CAROLINA

Mt. Mitchell

Silver Mt. Ridge

Crabtree Falls

Emerald Mine

McKinney Mine

Little Switzerland

Blue Ridge Mountains

TOE RIVER VALLEY

Drawn By Paul W. Porterfield
From Outline Map By Mark Sheppard

CABINS IN THE LAUREL

CHAPTER

I

Apalatcy

As you climb to the Toe River country in the North Carolina mountains from Marion and the hot rolling cornfields of the Piedmont, the bony slopes of Linville Mountain lie to the right. Away to the left Mount Mitchell, on the southern end of the Black Range, sprawls widely along the sky in a flattened curve like a giant tomato. The Black Brothers crowd next, partly shoving the loftier Mitchell into the background so that it seems lower than it is. Then the sky line skips fancifully over Potato Hill, dives into Deep Gap, runs evenly *BUCK CREEK* along Deer Ridge, and slides down Celo on the other end of the range to rest on the point of Bowlen's Pyramid.

The mountain wall is directly ahead, and the road dodges through coves and around hills that cut off the prospect of the high mountains. It doubles on itself with amazing dexterity and gallops up long grades at the only possible angle. At a curve the slope edges back to make room for a weathered cabin with a porch at the front running the length of the building. Short-legged, home-made chairs with two-slat backs and hickory-bark seats sit along the wall. The yard is bare of grass, tramped down hard, and swept clean with a home-made broom, making incongruous islands of the flowers and shrubs. A mountain woman finds some time to work with flowers no matter

The water-wheel still grinds the corn on the Toe River

how much she has to do. Under a tree by the side of a tiny branch an iron kettle hangs over a pile of ashes close by two tubs on a wash bench. Across the road the cornfield slants steeply to a stony creek that skirts a cliff.

At the next turn the door of a rude powder magazine opens abruptly into a rocky bank. Beyond, a new bungalow perches on stilts as though it had stopped to rest on its way down hill and someone had thoughtfully propped it up. A basement is not necessary where a cold snap lasts but three or four days.

The road scallops around and up more agilely than ever. As the car climbs the steep grade from Wildacres, the first view of Table Rock, dominating the eastern ridge line, flashes through the trees. That is the last hard pull. The altitude is gained and the road lopes easily along under the rim of the Blue Ridge. Two hundred feet below under the shade of a pine tree a log cabin snuggles into a laurel thicket. Another perches on a knoll out beyond. The whole panorama of the tangled road through the foothills lies knotted below. On the green slopes below the road the tree-tops are like nodding green feathers.

And then the details fade out before the magnificent sweep of space and mountains and sky from the high, open road of Little Switzerland. Black mountains surge up in the foreground; purple ones behind, with the mist boiling up gently between; rosy ones beyond them, and blue and gray ones; and on and on to the faint silver line of the last range etched on a shimmering fluid of gold and blue.

Wild locust, sourwood, oak, tulip poplar, chestnut, and pine slip past on rocky cliff and steep shoulder, crowding the tangles of laurel. There has been a riot of flowers since early spring as one shrub and then another picked itself out of the landscape, made its bow, and faded back into the green jungle. First the shad, like ghosts, then the whitening dogwood, the locust, azalea flaming in the shade, the pink masses of laurel like a fairy wedding, and then the dramatic rhododendron.

Suddenly the road dips from the ridge line and enters the Toe River country by Gillespie Gap where the Backwater men scrambled down the Blue Ridge on their way to meet Ferguson at King's Mountain. The Toe River Valley lies close to the Tennessee line in a pocket between the Blue Ridge, the Iron Mountains, and the lofty, balsam-topped range of the Blacks. From the Tennessee side one enters the Valley by a winding road that slides between the Yellow Bald and the main crest of the Blue Ridge, beyond which lies the

Linville country and Blowing Rock. Asheville and the Great Smokies lie to the southwest.

Toe River is the white man's contraction of Estatoe, the name of the Indian chief's daughter who drowned herself in the river when her lover, a tribal enemy, was killed as he attempted to carry her away in his canoe. In the high wooded valley behind the barriers the north and south branches of the river dodge through the laurel and rhododendron of the lesser ridges to come together at Toecane and form the Nolichucky. Toe River forms an integral part of the Tennessee Valley Power plan with reservoir storage dams in project at Celo and Micaville on the South Toe and on Rose's Branch and Loven's Creek, tributaries of the North Toe.

The high, protected Valley is a region of luxurious growth and abundant rainfall, with a mild climate except on those winter days when the altitude gets the better of the latitude and the wind howls down off the mountains. Up and down the criss-cross ridges and in the narrow coves the mountain people farm small holdings; grub out the laurel, endlessly clearing new land; market the big timber; and mine for mica, feldspar, and kaolin. Modern mining operations in the Valley date from 1867, but somebody made successful excavations three hundred years earlier. The mountain people call these first miners, whose identity is shrouded in mystery, "the ann-cients," and let it go at that.

In the mining excitement of the '70's and '80's, when people discovered that the ancient workings were apt to lead to a mica vein, they opened them up, and the new shafts destroyed the smaller old ones. One excavation on Rich's Knob near the Horse Stomp, whose dump showed a rusty black rock instead of the familiar jumble of spar and mica, has been left untouched. The practice of pushing dead mules, horses, and dogs down the shaft, instead of burying them, has insured the excavation against the curious.

D. D. Collis' father, who died in 1927 at the age of 91, said that when he was a boy no one had any knowledge of who made the excavation. It was just one of the mysterious doings of the ancients. John McBee's grandfather, who lived at the Horse Stomp in 1850, said that in his time the oldest inhabitants in the district had no idea of the origin of the working or what the miners were looking for. The mystery generated a dread of the place that drove out D. D. Collis after he had explored a hundred feet in the heading thirty-five years ago. Later he went about twenty-five feet down the shaft, hanging to a

The yard is bare of grass, tramped down hard, and swept clean with a home-made broom, making incongruous islands of the flowers and shrubs

pole, but that was far enough. John McBee of Spruce Pine, raised on Rock House Creek, remembers that he and his brothers used to toss pebbles down the pit, but they were afraid to enter it.

If you leave the highway by the Switzerland Inn and take the mud road that leads to Crabtree and the Emerald Mine, it will lead you down through close laurel shade and up over windy hilltops to a steep grass-grown trail that climbs Rich's Knob through a sunny slashing. The opening of the shaft at the Horse Stomp is on the southeast side of the Knob and about 500 feet below the top, with Grassy Creek Divide and Stony Knob beyond the cove in front. Star flowers, giant pink and white trilliums, mandrake, and lilies-of-the-valley cover the leaf mold of the slope and dot the rocky knoll of the dump that juts southward to fall away abruptly where the collapsed heading zig-zags in a leafy trough through a jungle of blackberry briers, second growth cherry, birch, and dead chestnut. The first workers carried the heading about four hundred feet toward the shaft, turned slightly and cut directly to it. The tunnel has collapsed to the point where it runs under the highest part of the

The whole panorama of the tangled road through the foothills lies knotted below

dump. Apparently the last few feet, communicating with the lower part of the shaft, are still intact. The heading must have been at least seven hundred feet long. D. D. Collis remembers that the mouth of the tunnel was still open twenty years ago, when he was cutting timber and used to sit by it to eat his dinner.

The pit measures about eighteen feet across, with the shaft proper approximately eight feet square. The opening is piled with light dry branches through which a wall of black rock is visible eight or ten feet down. The early workers had to dig through this solid ledge, possibly by prying open fissures, before they could sink the shaft. D. D. Collis says that beyond the rocks, beginning some fifteen to eighteen feet below the surface, there was a cribbing of chestnut logs. He does not know exactly how deep the shaft went, but it extended at least seventy or eighty feet.

The material on the dump consists of Carolina gneiss, impure quartz, and a gossan without visible trace of copper stain. The quartz vein must have carried the mineral the ancients sought, evidently gold, inasmuch as the absence of peacock pyrites, covellite, or copper stain on other dump material precludes copper, the other possibility. The extent of the workings would

Up and down the crisscross ridges the mountain people farm small holdings

indicate that the "ann-cients" found what they were looking for; miners would hardly run a seven hundred foot heading and sink a deep timbered shaft unless they were in ore.

Except in this one operation, the first workers in the Toe River Valley did little hard rock mining. They contented themselves with the upper decomposed mica at the Sink Hole mine, seven miles from Bakersville. Will Robinson, part owner of the Sink Hole, who has lived near it all his life, will take a visitor from one end to the other of the thick underbrush that obscures the early excavations, leaning on his tall staff while he points out where the ancients missed the vein, gave up, and tried it again. In the sunny cornfield that skirts the pits the earth sparkles with mica and the dusty corn tips up the little shining planes that catch the sun like splinters of looking glass. He says that the workings resembled a large railway cut, before the original form was broken by cave-ins and subsequent operations. They extended about a third of a mile along a ridge measuring from sixty to eighty feet across at the top, appearing originally to have been a series of concentric holes, like inverted cones, carried only deep enough to permit a spiral path to ascend the sides.

When General Clingman opened the workings in 1867, looking for silver,

*D. D. Collis remembers that the mouth of the tunnel was still open
twenty years ago*

there was plenty of evidence that people of a high order of intelligence had worked there extensively over a considerable time. He reported finding a slab near one of the pits, marked with the blows of an iron tool, but the only implements found in the diggings are flattened stone picks, five or six inches long and two or three inches broad. Plain marks of their use are visible in the sides of the mine banks when the loose dirt that sifted over them is removed.

As soon as the channels of the ancient operations are left behind—choked as they are by tangled brush and trees that disguise the contour—the increased firmness of the soil is apparent. The dirt removed from the original mines has never settled together thoroughly and yawns away from tree roots. General Clingman noted finding timber on the dumps with three hundred rings of growth, and Charles D. Stewart of Pineola, who dug to a depth of forty-two feet in one of the highest of the holes, found a tree bole of the same age.

The Hawk and Clarissa mines on Cane Creek, which appear to have been opened during the same period, show similar vestiges of the early excavations: pine logs found at a depth of thirty feet, the clear imprint of pine needles on clay in the Hawk mine opened by Carter Buchanan, and a large open-face cut with big trees in the pit and on the dump in the Clarissa. In 1896 a chestnut tree that measured twelve feet in circumference three feet above the ground was standing on the waste removed by the early miners.

The theory has been advanced that these first workers were moundbuilders, inasmuch as red rum mica had been found buried in their graves. But any excavations by moundbuilders would have been made three hundred years earlier than the period of the mining operations, before the land was even occupied by Indians; and also, there were no moundbuilders in North Carolina, although in Georgia there are transition mounds which appear to indicate some connection with the Cherokees. In the known historical period the Catawbas held the land to the crest of the Blue Ridge, and the Cherokees the land to the west. The Toe River Valley was a mutual hunting and fighting ground but had no Indian villages.

It is commonly believed in the district that the red rum mica in a museum in Madrid is identical with the peculiar type and quality that comes from Sink Hole. The Indians themselves said that "white men came from the south on mules and carried away a white metal." That points to the Spaniards in Florida.

F. A. Sondley, in his *Asheville and Buncombe County*, expresses no doubt of the Spanish occupation of North Carolina during the hundred and fifty years from 1540 to 1690. He believes that De Soto, after leaving Tampa Bay in Florida, marched northward through Georgia, South Carolina, and into North Carolina. "Then he turned west into the mountains, probably through Hickory Nut Gap to the French Broad River, and pursued in 1540 his journey toward the southwest until he came to the Mississippi. The chief object of his search was gold." He is supposed to have turned westward over the mountains at Xuala* in the country of the Sara or Suala Indians. "From the narrative of Garcilaso the Sara must then have lived in the piedmont region about the present line between South Carolina and North Carolina, southeast of Asheville. . . . Garcilaso in 1540 describes the village of Xuala as situated on the slope of a ridge in a pleasant hilly region, rich in corn and all the other vegetables of the country. In front of the village ran a stream which formed the boundary between the Xuala tribe and that of the Cofachiqui. This may have been either the Broad River or the Pacolet. . . . The first day's journey was through a country covered with fields of maize of luxuriant growth. . . . During the next five days they traversed a chain of easy mountains, covered with oak and mulberry trees, with intervening valleys, rich in pasturage and irrigated by clear and rapid streams. These mountains were twenty leagues across and quite uninhabited." They came at last to "a grand and powerful river" and a village at the end of a long island, where pearl oysters were found.

Dr. Sondley comments that this was unquestionably the Tennessee, which is formed by streams taking their rise in the mountains west of the Broad and Pacolet Rivers and whose waters still yield pearls of merchantable quality. He concludes, "Now it would be impossible for an army on the Broad or Pacolet River within one day's march of the mountains to march westward for six days, five of which was through mountains, and reach the sources of the Tennessee or any other river, without passing through Western North Carolina."

It is known that Don Luis de Velasco, as Viceroy of New Spain, sent out an expedition in 1559 under Luna y Arellano to establish a colony in Florida. One of his lieutenants went into Alabama in 1560, and Charles Jones in his *Hernando de Soto* says the expedition penetrated into the Valley River in

*"This Xuala of the Spaniards is the Suala of Lederer, Suali of the Cherokees and Cheraw of later writers."

The Toe River Valley is a region of luxuriant growth and abundant rainfall

Black mountains surge up in the foreground

Georgia. But there is no Valley River in Georgia, while there is a river of that name in Cherokee County, North Carolina, just over the much-questioned line between the states. Recalling the long dispute over that portion of the boundary and the considerable time when no one knew for certain where the line did lie, one realizes the probability that Jones erroneously supposed the river to be in Georgia. The evidences of gold mining in Cherokee County at least three hundred years ago are unmistakable. The Cherokees say that many years ago white men mined there throughout three long summers until they were killed by the Cherokees themselves. In 1564 Admiral Coligni sent a colony of Huguenots to Florida and tried to effect a settlement there under the leadership of René G. Laudonnière, but Pedro Menendez swooped down from San Felipe and broke it up. However, Laudonnière during his short stay was able to collect considerable silver from the Indians, who said they got it from the mountains of Apalatcy where there was also "redde copper." In 1653 an expedition from Virginia into North Carolina under Francis Yardley's patronage learned from the Tuscarora Indians of a wealthy Spaniard living with his family of thirty members and eight Negro slaves in the

The road doubles on itself with amazing dexterity

principal Indian town. He had resided there for seven years, and the Hay-
nokes or Eno Indians had "valiantly resisted the Spaniard's further northern
attempts" in North Carolina. Sir William Berkeley, Governor of Virginia,
expected to find silver mines in North Carolina when he sent John Lederer, a
German, into the country on an exploration trip in 1670, "for certaine it is
that the Spaniard in the same degrees of latitude has found many." Lederer
learned from the Usheries (Catawbas) and some visiting Sara Indians "that
two days' journey and a half from hence to the southwest, a powerful nation
of bearded men were seated, which I suppose to be Spaniards, because the
Indians never have any." Twenty years later James Moore, secretary of the
colony settled at Charleston in South Carolina, made his way through the
back country to the mountains, until he came to a place where his Indian
guides said that "twenty miles away Spaniards were mining and smelting
with furnaces and bellows."

Recent excavations in Cherokee County, the district richest in traces of
ancient mining activity, seem to bear out the Spanish hypothesis. In 1913
William R. Dockery of Marble explored a mine with timbering apparently

similar to that in the Horse Stomp on the mountain east of Tomatla, in the heart of the region where in recent years considerable gold has been mined in the river bed and along the banks of the Valley River. An old man named Palmer was in possession of directions, given him by an Indian, which purported to lead to a mine. There was nothing on the spot where the Indian told him to dig but a forked chestnut about fifteen inches thick, with dirt levelled to the trunk. Dockery, working with the old man's three boys, felled the tree and dug out the stump, whereupon they discovered a shaft eight feet square cribbed with oak timber at three foot intervals, banked against cave-ins and joined with mortice and tenon. They explored to a depth of sixty-four feet, when water filled the shaft. However, they had no difficulty in sinking an iron pipe seventeen feet lower through loose talc below the water level. The next year Dockery came upon a tunnel leading to another shaft on the ridge above. Near-by he discovered two other shafts of similar type, one of them sunk through solid rock. The oldest settlers believed that the ridge above these shafts and tunnels, where bones, beads, and arrowheads in unusual numbers have been picked up, was the site of a battle between Spaniards and Indians. There is also the story of an old furnace of unknown origin, now destroyed by the excavation for a cellar, and a Spanish coin mold found near-by.

Whoever the ancients were, they vanished from the Toe River country at least three hundred years ago, leaving surprisingly little more than the mine holes and the dumps. After that, the land was uninhabited except for the occasional passage of Cherokee hunters and warriors.

CHAPTER

II

Pole Cabins on the Toe

The Cherokees and the Catawbas, behind the ramparts of the Blue Ridge, got along better with the English King than with the colonists. Early in the century, when there was plenty of cheap low-country land, the white men did not want the rugged Indian country; but as the colony filled up, squatters began to overflow into the hills, until by 1763 the King, who had found the Cherokees and the Catawbas a convenient buffer against Louisiana during the recent war with France and Spain, thought it best to cement their allegiance by a specific guarantee to respect the Indian hunting grounds. From 1763, by royal edict, the mountains were closed to white settlers.

The Indians repaid the Crown's protection by active loyalty during the Revolution, swooping down from the hill country in a series of massacres which called for a determined campaign by the patriots before the border settlements were safe. The colonial government of the patriots retaliated in 1778 by throwing the Indian country open for settlement. It was an empty gesture unless they won the war. If Colonel Ferguson had been content with subduing the lowland Carolinas, the story of the Revolution might have been different. As it was, he sent word beyond the mountains that unless the settlers swore allegiance to the Crown, he would come into their country and burn their homes. As soon as the Backwater men heard his threat, they stopped grubbing laurel and deadening timber for cornfields and started out with their long rifles to find Ferguson.

Eleven hundred and twenty mounted woodsmen under Colonels Campbell, Shelby, and Sevier broke camp at Sycamore Shoals near Elizabethton, Tennessee, on the morning of September 26th, 1780, and rode into the mountains to the Shelving Rock, a mile up Doe River from Roan Mountain Station. The cavalcade ate dinner on the Grassy Bald of the Roan the next day. There William Crawford and Samuel Chambers deserted to warn Ferguson at Gilbert Town of their advance. That night, the 27th, they camped on Bright's Trace at Bright's Spring. On the 28th they rode down Roaring Creek to Toe River, passed Samuel Bright's new clearing, followed the Toe to the present site of Spruce Pine, and halted two miles beyond at Catha's place on Grassy Creek. When they reached Gillespie Gap the next morning, the party divided, fearing ambuscade, because by this time the deserters could have reached Ferguson with the news of their advance. Campbell's Division followed the crest of the Blue Ridge over the present site of the Washburn tunnel, dropped off the south side, and camped in Turkey Cove near the junction of Armstrong and North Cove Creeks. The other wing camped about six miles up North Cove by the Honeycutt Branch. From there they crossed the south end of Linville Mountain and took the Yellow Mountain road down Paddie's Creek to the Catawba. The men in the Turkey Cove camp rode into the lowlands across the present site of Lake James.

When the woodsmen straggled back again, victorious after the engagement at King's Mountain, the hated Major Ferguson was dead. They had left him lying naked on the slope for the vultures to eat, but Elias Powell, a British officer, obtained permission from Colonel Campbell to bury him. The body was wrapped in a raw beef hide and interred along with the corpse of Virginia Sal, Ferguson's red-haired maid-servant, who was killed as she tried to help a wounded soldier to his tent. Afterward Lord Rawdon reported in his account of the battle, "A numerous army appeared on the frontier drawn from Nolichucky and other settlements beyond the mountains, whose very names had been unknown to us."

Although Samuel Bright, who watched the Backwater men troop past his cabin on their way to King's Mountain, had the first homestead in the Valley, his was not the first land grant. The earliest entries filed under the Colonial Act of 1778, which opened the hill country to white settlers, were made by

The South Toe River skirts the lower slopes of the Black Range

speculators who did not intend to live on the land. Apparently the first of these went to Alexander, McKnitt, and Sharpe, who took out lands on the 10th of December of the year 1778. An entry for 400 acres "on Cane Creek [joining] the waters of Toe River and on both sides the path leading from Turkey Cove to Nolichucky and including the forks of said Creek" was approximately the present site of Bakersville. Their second grant, entered the same day, called for 100 acres "on North side Toe River [by] an old Indian path which crosses below the mouth of Rock Creek, on a large creek falling into Toe River on the west side including a large bottom and an island in said river." The reference seems to indicate the island near Jack's Creek in Yancey and the present site of Green Mountain Station. The same day that Alexander, McKnitt, and Sharpe received grants, Charles Reese took title to 140 acres "on South side Towe River between the second and third fords on the road from Turkey Cove to Nolichucky." A grant to William Lavender, August 7, 1787, calls for "250 acres in our county of Burke and Grassy Creek. Beginning at a white oak below the meadows on the west side of the Creek near the path that leads over the Iron Mountain." The land referred to in the Lavender grant is probably the present site of the S. T. Henry farm at Grassy Creek.

These early speculation grants were modest enough. Later entries covered enormous tracts, and their partition and the litigation they have entailed will serve to complicate Toe Valley records for years to come. William Cathcart took out 99,200 acres in the Toe River country on July 20, 1795, and another tract of 8,760 acres the same day on Rock Creek adjoining his Toe River survey. He followed his first entries with two more, July 20, 1796, one for 59,000 acres, and one for 16,000 acres on the Nolichucky. The Cathcart lands are still in the hands of the heirs. Waightstill Avery's name began to appear on large entries. In 1796 Blount of Beaufort had the largest entry of all, 320,640 acres, practically the whole of Avery County. Later it was sold for taxes and bought by John Strother. Land sold for five cents an acre, and at that figure the land grabbers usually stretched their boundary surveys to the limits of possibility.

Samuel Bright's homestead grant of March 15, 1780, calls for 640 acres of land on the Toe River near Humpback Mountain. He seems to have been satisfied with that until sixteen years later, when he added 100 acres more on Humpback Mountain, followed by another hundred on both sides of the river. The Brights did not remain long on Toe River. The story runs that a

In the Toe River Valley the hound is a member of the family

large family named Grant, from the Yadkin Valley, started to go through the mountains westward by the Yellow Mountain Gap. It was a large caravan, travelling with sheep and cattle, the men armed. They spent a night at the Bright cabin and started to go on. But it was late autumn, and the travellers ran into such bad weather that they turned back to the cabin again. There they were snowed in. Samuel Bright had a large family; so did the Grants. During the winter there were several marriages, and by spring the two families were so interlocked that the Grants persuaded the Brights to go west with them. Thus the name passed out of Valley history.

The land left behind by the Bright family was taken up by William Wiseman, the progenitor of the numerous Avery and Mitchell county Wisemans, who came into the country with William Pendley and William Davis. He was born in London, where, as a small boy, he was apprenticed to a wood worker. One morning in 1746 he dressed up in his best clothes and in company with two other half-grown boys, stowed away on a ship bound for America, where everyone could make a fortune. When the ship's captain discovered the three stowaways, he followed the usual custom of the time in such matters and sold them for indentured servants after the ship docked in Boston. A blacksmith bought Bill Wiseman for eight dollars.

The boy determined that his service in the smithy should be as brief as possible. In spare moments he set about carving a set of panther's legs for a table, the handsomest pattern he had so far learned from his master back home. The panther's foot held a smooth ball which he knew how to cut free of the grasping claws so that it rolled like a wheel and permitted the table to be moved easily. When the legs were finished, he sold them for enough to buy his freedom, a handsome price in those days. At last he was footloose to pursue his adventures. Boston was too much like London. Pennsylvania and Virginia were too settled. Eventually he drifted into the woods hemmed in by the high mountains in the Toe River country, and then he knew he had found the right place. His kinfolks remember that "old Billy was a quare feller. Couldn't plow a straight row of corn for always thinkin' how to make new wood pieces."

In 1790 there were eighty families located in the Valley, numbering about three hundred people. The Wisemans and Davenports were already settled at the foot of Yellow Mountain when André Michaux went through the district on his botanical expedition to collect rare plants for the palace at Versailles in 1794. The names of Abel Simpkins, James Ainsworth—who made claim for

200 acres "including McFalls improvement" and thereby takes his place in Valley annals as one of the first claim-jumpers—William Bright, Joseph Dobson, William Caruthers, Charles and David Baker appear in the records before 1800. The Baileys came up from Wilkes County at the turn of the century and settled near Bowditch.

A wagon train from Georgetown, Maryland, made up of the Silvers, Buchanans, Griffins, and Ellises, camped on Big Crabtree Creek on Christmas Eve in 1806. In the morning, when they found the snow blowing in their faces, they decided they had gone far enough. They found land that suited them in the vicinity of Little Crabtree and settled down to their clearing.

There was a young single woman in the party named Ruthia Ellis. Her sister had died on the journey, leaving three orphan children, the eldest of whom was six years old. When the travellers broke up into homestead groups, the three children went with Ruthia Ellis. She had to face the hard living in a new country with three dependents, but her courage was good, so good that when she saw a spot near the present site of Estatoe—a place that she liked better than the Little Crabtree lands—she moved there and started for herself, almost ten miles from her people. John Bailey, of the Bailey family at Bowditch, was a single man, but hopelessly bashful. He used to walk the twelve miles from his home to the pointed mountain at the bend of the North Toe and look down at the girl's little cleared patch in the thickets. Before he went back he would sally down and leave on the door stone a pair of wild turkeys, or half a venison, or maybe a string of fish. It was quite a while before Ruthia discovered who her admirer was. When he overcame his shyness, she smiled upon his attentions. They were married, and the young husband assumed responsibility for the three small Buchanans. John Bailey built a log house for his bride on the rounded ridge below his hunting ground in what is now called the sheep-meadow, fixed a pen for his cattle close to the house where the wolves could not get them, and claimed what became the Deer Park Lands, sometime in 1810.

He had hunted the Peak so thoroughly during his courtship that it gradually took his name. In the mountains one does not forget the old ones who have gone. Bailey's Peak for John Bailey, a green wooded point from the Ledger side, more softly curved from the Burnsville road. He hardly needs the printed page for remembrance who has a mountain to stand for him.

The Wilsons made homesteads on Cane Creek; the Penlands took up land

A log cabin snuggles into a laurel thicket

along the River between Pine Mountain and Art'ur's Knob, named for Art'ur McFall who hunted there. On November 29, 1814, Frederick Link bought a 150 acre tract on the Toe River which included all the hillside of Spruce Pine on the south bank, where the English Inn and the Harris High School were later to be situated. The Blalocks got the other side of the river now occupied by the business section of the village. Jonas Mace acquired a holding on Silver Run near the present Spruce Pine golf course.

Up and down the Valley the new settlers grubbed out clearings in the laurel and rhododendron thickets, girdled the big trees with deadening rings, and planted their corn fields. There was an abundance of deer, beaver, bear, otter, and wild turkey in the woods. The streams were full of fish. Hunters and trappers could get two dollars apiece for beaver skins, a dollar for deer, and from three to five dollars for otter. The ginseng root that grew wild sold for seven cents a pound. André Michaux, the French naturalist, taught the settlers how to prepare it for the Chinese market, when he came to the Valley to climb the Yellow Mountain. Each holding was practically self-supporting. Hides, corn, and honey could be bartered for salt and black powder. The

A bucket of water is kept handy on the porch

settlers raised everything else. If a man needed extra help, he called in his neighbors and repaid the service when they called on him.

From 1778 to 1791 the settlers of the whole region went to court at Morganton, a two-day trip each way. Then Buncombe County was formed, taking in a slice of the Toe River Valley land, and residents south of the Toe River and west of Crabtree Creek rode forty miles over bad roads to court in Asheville. Those north of the river still walked or rode horseback down the Blue Ridge to Morganton. The trail through the woods discouraged wagon travel. Whichever court the Valley residents attended, they received very little benefit from its sessions. The arm of the law was too short. Witnesses failed to appear for trials and justice was generally obstructed.

There were minor magistrates' courts in the Valley, however. The name of Samuel Bright's wife appears in one of the earliest sessions. William Wiseman, as presiding officer, awarded her thirty-nine lashes on the bare back for stealing a bolt of cloth from a peddler. Apparently the sentence was never executed.

The most sensational murder case in the history of the Toe River Valley was that of Frankie Silvers, accused of killing her husband, Charles Silvers. The defendant, who was tried in Morganton two years before county government was established in the Valley itself, was the first woman hanged in North Carolina. It is an old story of jealousy and revenge, played out in a cabin in the Deyton Bend of Toe River, a story that keeps turning over and over and adding to itself like a snowball. There are half a dozen versions. Here is one recently told to an outsider, which will serve to introduce the story and show how a tale metamorphoses with oral repetition.

THE QUILTIN'*

Away up under a mountain top
Where the ravens wheel and the low clouds drop
Lived Charlie Silvers and Frankie, his wife,
A lonesome, hungry sort of a life.

*In the mountains, nourished on the ballad tradition, verse, not prose, is the natural expression for a story, particularly a strongly rhymed, four-syllable measure. A practice joke, a wreck, a murder, anything that catches popular fancy and merits repetition, finds its way into verse. When I asked a man for the details of the race riot of 1923, he said he would give them to me the next day. In the morning he brought me the story of the riot in verse which he had composed in the interval. Sometimes people under religious excitement at revivals quote

He was tall and broad shouldered and thin as a brier
But Frankie was small like tough hay wire.
He fished and hunted and cleared the field;
She sowed and hoed and saved the yield,
Picked berries and cooked and wove and spun
And mostly finished what he had begun.
The cabin was old and far too small,
Not much of a shelter from rain at all.
The corn field tilted against the sky,
The land was ragged and rough and dry,
Too far from town to sell the crop
Away up under the mountain top.
The woman hated the lonely place
And longed for the fields at the mountain's base.
From the high bare knolls she watched them lie
All neat and fertile under the sky.
And Frankie was jealous. She nagged and spied
While she thought Charlie courted; she worried and cried
When he slipped away, now two days, now four.
Each time he came back she hated him more.
One time he was gone almost a week
Somewhere yon side of Bandana Creek.
It was late and Frankie had gone to bed.
She heard his step and raised her head.
"Who is it?" she called. "I'm back!" said he,
"Back home again. Got a bite for me?"
She cooked what there was, side-meat and pone.
Not much in the cabin when she stayed alone.
He stretched out to warm by the fire on the floor
And dropped off to sleep. But Frankie before
She went back to bed sat thinking. She knew
He would always run off when he wanted to

Scripture as though they were scanning. Because rhythm seems the natural form, I have put certain prose anecdotes into the strongly rhymed couplets of the country, giving, where possible, credit to the one who first told me the story. With the exception of The Quiltin', fictitious names have been substituted for those of the Toe River characters in all of my rhymed narratives in this book.

Bailey's Peak, a green wooded point from the Ledger side, more softly curved from the Burnsville road

And leave her alone. Well, she wouldn't stay.
She'd figure somehow to get away.
No one saw Charlie when he came.
If he disappeared, would she get the blame?
Close at hand the sharp axe stood.
She leaned above him. If she *should*—
The handle was heavy. The blade gleamed bright.
She brought it down with all her might.
Again! Again! She ran to the bed
And hid in the quilts till Charlie was dead.
So much was over and she had won,
But the horrible corpse—What must be done?
And gazing on him as he lay
She thought of a safe and awful way
To save herself and hide her crime,
To burn his body, a piece at a time.
And that she did,—all but his head;
She tied that up in a cloth instead.

Each small holding is practically self-supporting

It was too much Charlie to go in the grate.
You couldn't burn *all* of your lifelong mate.
But how to keep it? A ghastly sight.
She went outdoors. It was broad daylight
And the hollow stump of a sourwood tree
Yawned wide for Charlie hungrily.
She dropped him in. The deed was done
And where there were two there was only one.
One owned everything; one to spend,
One to sit worrying hours on end.
Day followed day—perhaps a week,
Then a boy came climbing the winding creek,
With word from Bertie McGuire, his mother,
If Frankie could get there some way or other,
She wished she'd come and help her quilt.
And Frankie was glad to go. The guilt
Of what she had done was mounting higher.
She'd eat cold food without a fire.

When she went out, all she could see
Was the hateful stump of the sourwood tree.
She went with the boy and forgot he was there,
Afraid on the mountain, she peered everywhere.
There were three of her friends at the quilting frame
In the midst of a ballad when Frankie came,
And Bertie said, "Come in and warm!"
With a friendly squeeze on her spindling arm.
The quilt on the poles was the Irish chain,
Of white and red like a bright blood stain.
The women asked what she had to tell,
And she said, "Nothin'. I don't feel well."
And they all sympathized and 'lowed she looked bad
And reviewed all the sickness they had had.
She hardly spoke as the hours dragged through.
Just sat and sewed as she came to do.
As they rolled the poles for the last chain star,
The milch cow mooed at the cow pen bar.
Then Bertie got up and poked the fire,
And threw on pine so the blaze leaped higher,
And cut some bacon to fry out the fat
And put it to cook; got her man's old hat
And her working clothes to milk the cow
Out doors in the cold, and that was how
The bacon sizzled and frizzled and burned,
When it should have been watched and lifted and turned.
The guests quilted on till they smelled the smoke,
And commenced to sneeze and cough and choke.
A woman dropped her needle and ran
To snatch from the blaze the smoking pan.
They opened the door and fanned out the smell
As much as they could, and went out to tell
With laughter how they had talked so much
They forgot the bacon and fire and such,
But Frankie was silent and stayed behind
Distracted with something on her mind.

Wild locust, sourwood, oak, tulip poplar, chestnut, and pine crowd the tangles
of laurel on rocky cliff and steep shoulder

She sat on the hearth and held her head,
And thought of Charlie, burnt and dead,
And how his smoke had rolled and hung,
And curled and swirled and billowed and swung.
The same black smoke clouds in the air;
The same burnt smell was everywhere.
The hateful stench was making her sick.
She wanted to go and go right quick
And feared the smell would follow too;
She feared the woods that the trail wound through.
She dreaded the sight of the sourwood tree
Where Charlie's head waited gruesomely.
She feared the vengeance of the Lord
Might make her tell of her own accord.
If he cared enough to make her pay
He might have picked this special day

That's how they used to build the old houses

And caused Himself that burning smell,
To terrify, and make her tell.
The rest came back. She could not rise.
She did not dare to face their eyes.
Her wraps lay yonder on the bed,
But back at home was Charlie's head.
She could not stay. She dared not go.
She rocked, wild eyed, and cried, and so
At last she told how Charlie died,
And it came out, though no one spied
When piece by piece she fed the flame
With human flesh. The awful shame
Of Frankie's deed spread to every glen
Where stood the homes of mountain men.
Her friends forsook her. The Law stepped in
And Frankie hung for her heinous sin.
And they still tell when bacon's fried
Too long and scorched, how Charlie died.

The steep hillside behind the cabin is overrun by a dense undergrowth that appears to have stood there forever

In her ninetieth year Aunt Cindy Norman, sister of the murdered man, gave W. W. Bailey, of Spruce Pine, the following account of the killing.

In the winter of 1831 Charles Silvers was living in the Deyton Bend with his wife, Frankie, and their baby daughter. Very early on the morning of December 23rd Frankie dropped in at her father-in-law's and found the family preparing to wash. "My washing is done and I've scoured too," she boasted, and her mother-in-law marvelled at her smartness to do a day's work before dawn. Frankie went on to tell the reason for her visit. Charlie had gone over the river on the ice the day before for his Christmas liquor, and had not returned. She was worried and begged his people to look at the crossings to see if he had fallen through. They searched the river for a considerable distance, but there was neither trail nor break in the ice. When he was still absent after several days, other families joined in the search. Frankie shook the valley with her lamentations. Word of the strange disappearance seeped into the country around Bear Creek and Art'ur's Knob.

An old man named Jakie Collis determined to go and walk over the ground himself to satisfy his curiosity on certain points. He went first to the father's house, where Cindy Silvers, the eight-year-old sister of the lost man, offered to take him to Charlie's empty cabin. Frankie had by now given up on his return and refused to stay there alone with her grief. At the deserted cabin Jakie and Cindy and others who had joined them scrutinized closely the mantel and sides of the fireplace. There were fresh irregular chippings at intervals over the whole surface where someone had hewn lightly with an axe. It gave Jakie an idea.

"Help me lift the puncheons," he said to one of the men.

The upper surface of the slabs was neatly scoured, but the rounded sides underneath were streaked at the cracks with old blood stains. There was a fresh layer of ashes between the puncheons and the earth. Old Jakie thrust his hand into them and found them clotted with what appeared to be dried blood. Just then Frankie, who had watched from a distance, pushed her way among the men like a mad woman and ordered them off. The men stood still, looking at her with horror in their eyes that told her what they suspected. Then they went on with their work. In a frenzy of despair she wept and swore and made wild protestations while she saw the men sift the ashes in the fireplace and find human teeth and the remains of bones showing hack marks. Somebody realized that the big pile of hickory wood that had stood by the door was gone. When they looked at the axe, its edge was dulled with chopping something other than wood. The facts were plain enough without Frankie's extraordinary behavior. They sent for the sheriff to take charge of her.

More evidence came to light as the weather grew warmer. The investigation of a hollow sourwood where a dog sniffed suspiciously revealed the intestines and other parts of the body that did not burn readily. The horror of the tragedy shook the Valley from end to end.

Judge Donnell sentenced Frankie to death at the June term, 1832. She appealed, but Judge Ruffin sustained the conviction. When there was no hope through the regular channels of the law, her kinfolks took a hand in the affair. They spirited her out of jail and took her through the streets in a load of hay. As soon as they were out of town, Frankie climbed off the wagon. Dressed in a man's clothes and carrying a gun, she tramped behind the hay. The sheriff's posse overtook the suspicious load too quickly for her to crawl back out of sight. She tried to brazen it out.

"Want to buy some hay?" she asked in the deepest possible voice.

"No. We don't want hay," answered the sheriff, helping himself to the gun. "But we do want you, Frankie."

It was no use. She went back to jail. In the beginning she had protested her innocence. Now when there was no hope she made full confession.

According to her story she had been goaded by jealousy to kill her husband, and was awaiting the first opportunity to do it. On the night of December 22nd, he came into the house tired and cold from a day spent chopping wood to last over Christmas. He had a big pile of hickory chunks laid by to show for his labor. After supper he took the baby in his arms and lay down on a sheepskin in front of the fire to get the chill out of his bones. The axe lay handy, and in her anger she longed to seize the chance to kill him. In case she should find courage to go through with it, she gently slid the sleeping baby out of his arms. He did not waken.

At last, to end the torment of indecision, she seized the axe and tried to sever his head from his body in one mighty stroke. The blow glanced, and Charlie, horribly mutilated, sprang up and thrashed about making noises that frightened her half to death. She jumped into bed and covered her head to shut out the sound until he commenced to grow quieter from loss of blood. There was no way but to go on with it now. When she could muster courage, she got out of bed and struck the blows that quieted him forever. The rest of the night she spent dismembering and burning the body. It took a hot fire, and in a single night she used the whole of the Christmas hickory. Then in that blazing, suffocating cabin she carefully whittled away the spatters of blood and grease from the mantel and sides of the fireplace and scoured every stain from the floor that had been generously smirched as the body thrashed about. She washed the spattered bedding. That was the washing of which she boasted to her mother-in-law a few hours later.

Frankie Silvers must have had some feeling, because in the last days of her imprisonment she contrived a long, gloomy poem which she recited from the scaffold before her execution, July 12, 1833.

THE FRANKIE SILVERS SONG

On one dark and dreary night
I put his body out of sight.
To see his soul and body part
It strikes with terror to my heart.

I took his blooming days away,
Left him no time to God to pray,

And if sins fall on his head
Must I not bear them in his stead?

The jealous thought that first gave strife
To make me take my husband's life.
For days and months I spent my time
Thinking how to commit this crime.

And on a dark and doleful night
I put his body out of sight;
With flames I tried him to consume
But time would not admit it done.

You all see me and on me gaze—
Be careful how you spend your days
And ne'er commit this awful crime,
But try to serve your God in time.

Judge Daniel has my sentence passed
These prison walls I leave at last;
Nothing to cheer my drooping head
Until I'm numbered with the dead.

But O, that dreadful Judge I fear;
Shall I that awful sentence hear?
"Depart, ye cursed, down to Hell,
And forever there to dwell."

I know that frightful ghosts I'll see,
Gnawing their flesh in misery,
And taken and there attended be
For murder in the first degree.

Then shall I meet that mournful face
Whose blood I spilled upon this place,
With flaming eyes to me he'll say,
"Why did you take my life away?"

His feeble hands fell gently down,
His chattering tongue soon lost its sound.
My mind on solemn subjects rolls

He will work the land his great-grandfather worked

A weathered cabin with a porch at the front running the length of the building

My little child—God bless its soul;
All you that are of Adam's race
Let not my faults this child disgrace.

Farewell, good people, you all now see
What my bad conduct brought on me;
To die of shame and disgrace
Before this world of human race.

Awful, indeed, to think of death,
In perfect health to lose my breath;
Farewell, my friends, I bid adieu,
Vengeance on me must now pursue.

Great God! How shall I be forgiven?
Not fit for earth, not fit for Heaven,
But little time to pray to God
For now I try that awful road.

Throughout her trial and imprisonment Frankie maintained a philosophic indifference. People whispered that she had not told all she knew; that some of her kinfolks helped her murder her husband and she was shielding them; that even as she mounted the scaffold, she expected a pardon. Everyone looked forward to a spectacular last moment development. At the top of the gallows steps Frankie indicated to the hangman that she wanted to say something. Now it was coming.

"Die with it in you, Frankie!" called her father from the crowd.

But Frankie was not going to tell anything more than everyone knew already. She wanted to read her poem. One story says that she had a piece of cake in her hand as she ascended the gallows platform. When the hangman asked if she were ready, she said that she would be when she finished eating her cake. Then Frankie Silvers pulled the black cap down over her face herself and shut out the daylight forever.

At that period it was the custom of the state to turn over a hanged man's body to medical students for dissection. There were many petitions for Frankie's body because a woman's corpse was hard to obtain. The father, harassed with the fear of such ignominy for his daughter, caused several graves to be dug before the execution, all of which were made into mounds by the following morning. Meanwhile he spirited the body away. The night after the execution it lay hidden under sacks in the barn of the Buck Horne Tavern ten miles from Morganton. Then it was secretly buried in a private burying ground nearby.

The words of the poem were eagerly seized upon by a countryside familiar with the dramatic story. It became a song, but it could be sung only when no members of either family were present, lest they be reminded of the tragedy. This is not a feud country, and while neither family took up the grudge, everyone felt that it was better not to meddle with fresh wounds. The song survives today in an eerie, mournful tune whose urgent minor beat is the restless scurrying of unlaid ghosts in lonely places.

III

Yancey County

The Toe River Valley became a complete political unit with a county government of its own in 1833. It had been the policy of the state government to set up new counties as soon as the population warranted it. By 1833 there were enough families in the Valley demanding a county government of their own to assure titles, build roads, and generally keep the peace. Yancey County was formed from lands subtracted from Burke and Buncombe counties.

Yellow Jacket John Bailey sold the Commissioners a hundred acres of land for the county seat, and the court acknowledged the deed in the June session of 1834. Everyone was well pleased with the central location of the county seat on the Burnsville plateau, equally hard to reach from all sections. Those who lived in the more thickly settled Rock Creek and Cane Creek settlements had farther to come, but the road was more level than for those who came through Ivy and Paint Gap. It all evened up agreeably.

The town was named Burnsville for Captain Otway Burns, Commander of the Privateer Snapdragon in the War of 1812. The first court, held in the Caney River meeting house on the third Monday in January, 1834, executed a good deal of business in spite of an offhand start the first day with sixteen justices and no chairman. However, that first day they elected the clerk,

Days of sunshine and sport along the branch

sheriff, solicitor, surveyor, registrar, entry-taker, county trustee, treasurer of public buildings, coroners, and processioners, to hold office until the regular election in July. They appointed constables and polling places and subsequently licensed David D. Baker and W. W. Carson to sell liquor by small measure "being men of good character and steadiness," created a commission to build a court house and gave it proper authority, and ended by fining the newly elected sheriff a gallon of cider, and Reuben Keith another gallon, and three dozen apples to go with it.

Yancey had a court house by 1836, and the pleasure-loving, turbulent population supplied plenty of business, with their drinking and fighting. In the spring term at Burnsville in 1837, out of fourteen criminal cases, ten were for affrays and assaults. At the fall term in 1840 there were fifty-five criminal cases, thirty-one of them for assaults. At the January term, 1844, two prominent citizens were fined for "having passed a contempt to the court by fighting at the court house door and in the presence of the court." In 1854 Judge A. S. Merrimon, holding court at Burnsville, deplored the heavy drinking of the office-holding class on the grounds that it kept them from doing their work properly. At least they kept the records better and with neater penmanship than in the period following 1900, when there are entries upside down, and books have been started and cast aside after only five or six pages have been used.

Sheriffs, who were also tax collectors, sometimes had a way of failing to turn over funds to the proper parties. In 1850 and again in 1858 the sheriff absconded. In 1855 the county chairman refused to make account of money entrusted to him, whereupon M. P. Penland was elected to the office to straighten things out. In 1859 Aden Wiseman discharged his share of the bond for the absconding sheriff of the year before by selling 1200 gallons of whiskey in Charlotte and Shelby. Land was beginning to be valuable in the Valley, and there was an epidemic of barefaced claim-jumping of the type initiated by Ainsworth forty years before. On December 28, 1836, Allen Sparks received fifty acres of land "on waters of Bare Creek including Clem Buchanan's improvement." David Baker claimed 100 acres of land in Yancey "including Jesse Typton's improvement" in December of 1838. The same year William Dixon and J. S. Young entered land on Grassy Creek "to include Bas Elkins' house-logs." As late as 1852 Newsome Mace took out 75 acres "on Rockhouse Creek near the head—including a turnip patch cleared by

Isaac McFalls." (The McFalls mentioned in the grant was his brother-in-law.) Land that had sold for five cents an acre now cost from twenty-five to fifty cents as the country filled up. In 1844 Thomas Clingman wrote in a letter that land suitable for sheep walks might be had for from one dollar to ten dollars an acre.

There was a fairly constant stream of travel eastward and westward that kept the hills in close touch with the low-country. Drovers herded hundreds of pigs, sheep, and cattle eastward over the mountains, destined for sale on the great tobacco and cotton plantations that raised more saleable products than food stuffs, and the travelling market stimulated a lively cattle, sheep, and hog business in the hill country itself.

If the Civil War had not destroyed the slave-holding system, Toe River Valley would quite possibly have become a great stock-raising country with a rich market lying at its feet.

Today the population of the Toe River country is four times as great as in 1850, but the number of cattle has not increased proportionately. The Department of Agriculture's figures for 1931 show only 4,170 swine as compared with 29,132 in 1850, and a fourth the number of sheep raised in that year.

A glance at the following table of livestock and grain production in the Toe River Valley in 1840 and 1850 shows how the district was forging ahead.

NUMBER, QUANTITY, OR VALUE PRODUCED

	1840	1850
Cattle	5,585	10,379
Sheep	5,041	20,061
Swine	18,718	29,132
Wool	2,931 lbs.	19,829 lbs.
Butter and Cheese	$ 5,182	$ 8,984.20
Rye	418 bu.	6,275 bu.
Corn	405,390 bu.	284,016 bu.
Tobacco	4,830 lbs.	12,245 lbs.
Oats	33,670 bu.	122,544 bu.
Potatoes	89,270 bu.	12,928 bu.

The mountain woman meets a stranger with reserved composure

Besides the through traffic eastward and westward, there was an active life belonging to the Valley itself. Trade in ginseng had decreased to $5,500 total sale in 1850 from the 86,000 pounds sold in 1837, but there was a constant market to take its place in bloodroot, raspberry leaves, liverwort, and spearmint. The immense tracts of woodland were not considered valuable except as potential clearings, and until 1850 the Valley needed but two sawmills. Roads were no worse in the mountains than anywhere else, and constant use kept the through trails to the Watauga settlement and the West in fair condition. By 1840 a road had been built from Burnsville to the crest of the Blue Ridge that was intended to link the county seat of Yancey with the Piedmont. After a number of false starts the McDowell and Yancey Turnpike Company and the Laurel Turnpike Company opened a toll road sometime about 1850. They charged the following rates:

Wagon with five or six horses	$.75
Wagon with four horses	.50
Pleasure carriage drawn by two horses	.75
Wagon with two or three horses	.30
Wagon or cart with one horse	.15
Peddler	.50
Gig or sulky	.25
Man and horse	.10
Loose horse or mule	.05
Cattle each	.03
Sheep and hogs	.01

Most of the present-day roads follow approximately the old trails.

In 1839 the Toe River Valley had voted against the state education system, but by 1844 the people decided to partake of the State Literary Fund. Probably the first schools in the Valley date from 1844. The following year Stephen Adams founded Burnsville Academy, the first private school in the district.

The population was far less illiterate in 1850 than in the dark period during and after the Civil War. In 1850 only 962 adults out of a population of 7,809 were unable to read and write, a little over twelve per cent of illiteracy. By 1853 there were twenty-two schools in session with a two and a half months term. The teacher received sixteen dollars a month. Everything about the log schools with their four-foot chimneys was contrived from

The mountain man chafes at a monotonous, comfortable job that involves no individual effort

materials closest at hand, benches of logs split open, the comparatively level side to sit on, the curved half turned underneath and bored with holes into which legs were inserted; ink of pokeberry and bead-bush boiled together; pens from goose quills; wood from the school yard to keep the fires going; and presiding over the hubbub of students spelling at the top of their lungs or reeling out multiplication tables from Fowler's arithmetic, the teacher with his hickory rod.

The total revenue in Yancey County for school purposes reached $2250.32 in 1860, of which $467.36 was left at the end of the year. Possibly one reason the school fund seldom ran dry is that no very great demands were made upon it. One gets a fairly good idea of what was considered sufficient for a practical education by looking over the Yancey court requirements laid upon guardians to assure the schooling of bond children.

Lewis Bailey, bound at the age of seven or eight until he should be twenty-one, was to receive eighteen months' schooling and at the end of his servitude, one horse, a bridle and saddle worth $65.00, and three good suits of clothes "one of which is to be store goods." When Thomas Sawyer was bound to Daniel Carter, the court directed the latter to give him two years of

Blaine Buchanan's house overlooks the Cane Creek Valley

schooling before he was fifteen years old and another year before the time of his freedom, as well as a horse, bridle, and saddle worth $80.00, three suits, one to be of good decent broadcloth. He was also to teach the boy the art of farming. In the fall term of 1843 James Boon was allowed the apprentice service of Amos Boon until he should come of age in return for two years of schooling, one horse, saddle, and bridle, worth $80.00, and four suits of clothes, two of which should be good "janes" and two of everyday stuff, an axe, a good hat, and "a pare of shoes."

A girl evidently needed less schooling. Polly Bailey, bound to Abner Jervis, was to receive only one year of schooling, but she would receive five suits of clothes, two to be of store goods, a cow, a calf, a bed, and some furniture. Then all she needed was a husband.

There were more churches than there were schools—twenty-nine of them in 1850—of which twenty were Baptist, eight Methodist, and one Dunkard. Ministers were scarcer than churches, and congregations followed their circuit-riding parsons from one community to another in their eagerness to hear him. On March 18, 1850, Lewis Buchanan, Isaac Cox, Thomas Sparks, and Christopher Rathbone entered fifty acres of land on the waters of Pine

Branch with the avowed purpose of building a meeting house, a grant unique of its kind in the state records. The site of the old church is the clearing in front of the Fred Shaffer property in Spruce Pine.

There are a few old men and women living in the Valley who remember the days before the war. Aunt Polly Boone, who says she is Daniel Boone's great-granddaughter, is so old she has lost count. She sits with staring, sightless eyes whose big black pupils appear to see as she restlessly holds a scrap of cloth on her knee, or plays with an acorn that flashes back and forth between her hands like a shuttle. Aunt Polly can see the old times if not the new. Going barefoot to the log churchhouse, with rags wrapped around her legs for warmth; "snakin' the beds" before she would dare crawl in between the covers; living in a new cabin in a wild country where one set up housekeeping with an axe, a gun, a kettle, and a pile of straw in the corner. The "painters" cried outside her cabin at night, and once she saw a bear carry off in his arms the sow they had been fattening for company.

She will tell you about the family who built a log cabin on a rock with a hole in it. It looked like a good place, because the floor was already made and the convenient hole was just the place to dump ashes without toting them out of doors. It was cold weather and the hole had received plenty of scoopfuls one night before the man and his wife went to bed. Later the woman awoke to feel something curling over the covers. Frightened, she roused her husband, and half-believing she dreamed it, begged him to make a light. As he stepped on the floor, something bit him before he could get to the hearth. The bed and floor were swarming with rattlesnakes. The cabin had been built over a snake den, and the snakes had been aroused by the warm ashes poured down the hole. The man died on the floor, the woman unable to leave the bed to help him. Keeping the snakes off herself with the quilts, she screamed until at last help came, and she was lifted from the room through a hole cut in the roof.

Uncle Zack McHone, a son of Kim McHone, from whom Spruce Pine took its early name "The Kim Thickets," is ninety years old, confined to bed with a broken hip that refuses to mend. He lives in a weathered cabin on Chalk Mountain above Spruce Pine, with a wide view of the Blue Ridge to the south and the Roan and Yellow Mountains spread out to the north.

"Look what Zack done!" he says, pulling himself up on his pillows to point at the fields beyond the open door. "I got good land and I got minerals. Spar and fluorspar, too. When I come hit was all woods. You kaint seem to

Aunt Polly Boone is so old she has lost count

make the young 'uns see the old times. There's folks all over everywhere now till you're like to tromp on 'em, and they all got it easy.

"You kaint know how simple we done in those days. Pickin' out of the cook pot and no plates and nothin' but wooden bowls. Spoons, we had, and a few things out of pewter. Most of the time we lived on corn bread, milk, butter, and meat. When we wanted pork, we shot a wild pig. The same with beef. Nobody penned up their animals. They turned 'em loose and when they needed meat they hunted 'em down. Men wore caps of rawhide. Pa tuck his and beat a man's face all to pieces once when they had a fight. Some folks had fur caps or 'most anything to cover their heads with. We wore flax and tow clothes mostly.

"My folks lived to start with over near Phil Tolley's on the Burnsville road in a place I could show you if I could just get up and walk. When we lived over there our house wa'n't finished for a long time. My daddy was an awful man to drink by spells and I know once when the chimney hadn't got no further than your shoulder and no floor laid but enough for the bed to stand on, he went off and didn't come back when night come. There was just two little girls then, the least one a baby, and the rest of us not born yet. Ma was scared because the wolves was gathering close and howling in the bushes, edging up as hit fell night. She kept running out in the clearin' for a rail and then another and back like the whole pack was after her, and she piled 'em around the bed where the young uns was, and she piled 'em in front of the door that wouldn't shut. Pappy didn't come and in the night the wolves fit and growled by the house, wantin' to come in, and Mammy seen their eyes shine in the fire light where they'd slunk under the floor that wa'nt half finished. And she'd have at 'em with a stick blazin' out of the fire (they don't dast go near fire) and then mornin' come and their scolding and yowling got farther and farther off.

"All the next day Pappy didn't come neither and hit started gettin' night and the wolves was gatherin'. Mammy couldn't stand no more. She was plum drug out. She just took the baby and set her straddle of her neck and crossed her legs under her chin and tied 'em tight and she grabbed my sister's hand and run for the Hoppas cabin that stood clean over the mountain in what's the Jase Burleson orchard now. She tuck the old Cane River Indian trail and run with the baby flapping on her back and when she come on the ridge she fell down and thought the varmints would git her. But they didn't and she got up and run on to Hoppas's."

Uncle Rube Mosley of Rock Creek remembers that "the varmints was getting clared out pretty well when I was a boy. Hit was a wild country for my pappy though. He was born back in 1822 and he was one of them that holp move the Indians from Crusaw Jack's Race Paths on Unicoi to the Hiwasee Purchase. Nathan was his name and there was thirteen of us children, six boys and seven girls. I was the fifth son. We'd made a house full if we'd all been home to one time, but of course some of the big ones had gone off by themselves and settled when there was still little ones comin'.

"We got along plain. The fireplace was six foot and took a big back-log that would burn two days in medium weather. Pap would haul it to the door and it would take four of us to get it to the fire. We'd lay down rollers of course. Then we'd light up a good blaze and roll up in sheepskins on the floor to sleep of a night."

W. W. Bailey recalled hearing his father, James Bailey, tell of the building of the Deer Park homestead after the death of his grandfather, John Bailey, the bashful hunter who married Ruthia Ellis. When James came home to Deer Park from his apprenticeship to a mechanic in Morganton, the family was living in a little log cabin in the sheep meadow. John Bailey was sick and had not been able to put out a crop. The son and daughter who stayed at home while James went to the low-country had married and gone for themselves. John and Ruthia had almost stripped the house to help them get started; there was not even an axe. Three weeks later John Bailey died, and James started out late with the planting.

When he had managed by hard work to make enough to live on, he commenced to plan for a house of his own. First, he had to make a cart with which to haul logs, something light because there was only a young colt to pull it. He cut the ends from a big log, bored and joined a straight tongue, and contrived a hook to fasten on the under side of the tongue, near the end so that it would not drop down and dig into the ground. That was his wagon. The white oak must be cut at a certain time of year or the worms would eat the fibre. He felled the logs in season, put one end on the little wheel carriage, and dragged them one by one to the present site of the house. The building was finished sometime in 1840. Then James Bailey paid court to Polly Cox, a neighbor's daughter, and married her.

The names of most of the outstanding mountains of the Toe River Valley date from the earliest settlers, but Mount Mitchell, which rears up on the sky line loftiest of all, waited until 1857 for the name it bears today. The series

Deer Park House retreats darkly among the trees

of events that determined the name of Mitchell's Peak has linked with the Toe River country the lives of three people, the mention of one of whom promptly suggests the other two: General Clingman, Professor Elisha Mitchell of the University of North Carolina, and Big Tom Wilson the bear hunter, a bluff mountain man from Caney River.

After André Michaux's scientific journey to the Valley in 1794, there was no other scholarly expedition of note until Thomas Clingman and Professor Mitchell appeared in 1844 to engage in a series of observations in the Balsams, the Smokies, and the Black Mountains. The Clingman-Mitchell dispute over the comparative height of two peaks in the Black Range arose out of their visit. Professor Mitchell maintained that the balsam-topped giant, locally called the Black Dome, was the highest mountain in the east, although its flattened ridge line was far less imposing than the angles of the twin-humped mountain next door, which Clingman believed to be the highest. Each man had measurements to prove his point.

The controversy dragged on until 1857, when Professor Mitchell determined to establish his claim and end the argument by re-measurement. In June he started running a series of levels from Morganton. Working alone, he plunged into the wilderness on Saturday, June 27th, expecting to meet his

Mount Mitchell used to be called the Black Dome

son at an appointed place in the Black Mountains the following Monday. When he failed to appear, the boy waited until Friday before he gave the alarm. Then there was a hue and cry all up and down Yancey County, until Big Tom Wilson found Mitchell's body sitting upright in a chilly grave at the bottom of a pool on a fork of Sugar Camp Creek. The scientist had evidently lost his bearings in the fog, slipped, and hurtled down the cataract. After ten days in the icy water the body was perfectly preserved.

By measurements taken before the accident Mitchell had established his point that the Black Dome was indeed the highest point east of the Mississippi. In the excitement over his tragic death the name was changed to Mount Mitchell. If Clingman came off second best, at least the peak next door was named for him, and in the next year, 1858, he carved out fame for himself in the Smokies with the exploration of the mountain that came to be Clingman's Dome.

Big Tom Wilson, already well known locally as a hunter and woodsman, became famous overnight; from the time of his discovery of Mitchell's body until his death, he was the most visited man in the Valley. When Charles Dudley Warner and a friend rode through the country in 1885 on their way to Asheville from Abingdon, Virginia, they stayed overnight at the Wilson cabin. The following day Big Tom guided them over Mitchell's Peak. Warner's book *On Horseback*, which gives an account of the journey, describes Wilson as living on a plantation having "an open-work stable, an ill-put together frame house, with two rooms and a kitchen, and a veranda in front, a loft and a spring house in the rear. . . . Some fish rods hung in the porch and hunter's gear depended on hooks in the passage way to the kitchen. In one room there were three beds, in the other two, only one in the kitchen. On the porch was a loom, with a piece of cloth in process.

"Big Tom Wilson, as he is known all over this part of the State, would not attract attention from his size. He is six feet and two inches tall, very spare and muscular, with sandy hair, long gray beard and honest blue eyes. He has a reputation for great strength and endurance; a man of native simplicity and mild manners. He joined us in our room after supper. This apartment, with two mighty feather beds, was hung about with all manner of stuffy family clothes, and had in one end a vast cavern for a fire. Talk? Why, it was not the least effort. The stream flowed on without a ripple. 'Why, the old man,' one of the sons confided to us next morning, 'can begin and talk right over Mount Mitchell and all the way back, and never make a break.'

The flattened ridge line of Mount Mitchell is less imposing than the angles of the twin-humped mountain next door

"Though Big Tom had waged a lifelong warfare with the bears, and taken the hide off at least a hundred of them, I could not see that he had any vindictive feeling towards the varmint, but simply an insatiable love of killing him, and he regarded him in that half humorous light in which the bear always appears to those who study him. As to deer—he couldn't tell how many of them he had slain. But Big Tom was a gentle man, he never killed deer for mere sport. With rattlesnakes, now, it was different. There was an entire absence of braggadocio in Big Tom's talk, but somehow, as he went on, his backwoods figure loomed larger and larger in our imagination. . . . But hunting and war did not by any means occupy the whole of Big Tom's life. He was also engaged in 'Lawin'.' He had a long time feud with a neighbor about a piece of land and alleged trespass, and they'd been 'lawin'' for years, with no definite result. . . .

"Long after we had all gone to bed, we heard Big Tom's continuous voice, through the thin partition that separated us from the kitchen, going on to his little boy about the bear; every circumstance of how he tracked him, and what corner of the field he entered, and where he went out, and his probable size and age, and the prospect of his coming again; these were the details of real every-day life, and worthy to be dwelt on by the hour. The boy was never tired of pursuing them. And Big Tom was just a big boy also in his delight in it all."

Warner's party started to climb Mount Mitchell the following morning about 7:30 o'clock.

"From Wilson's to the peak of Mitchell it is seven and a half miles; we made it in five and a half hours. A bridle path was cut years ago, but it has been entirely neglected. It is badly washed, stony, muddy, and great trees have fallen across it which wholly block the way for horses. . . . Those who have ever attempted to get horses over such ground will not wonder at the slow progress we made. Before we were half-way up the ascent, we realized the folly of attempting it on horseback; but then to go on seemed as easy as to go back.

"What a magnificent forest! Oaks, chestnuts, poplars, hemlocks, the cucumber (a species of magnolia, with a pinkish, cucumber-like cone), and all sorts of northern and southern growths meeting here in splendid array. And this gigantic forest, with little diminution in size of trees, continued two-thirds of the way up. . . . Half-way up, Big Tom showed us his favorite, the biggest tree he knew. It was a poplar, or tulip. It stands more like a column than a tree, rising high into the air, with scarcely a perceptible taper, perhaps sixty, more like a hundred, feet before it puts out a limb. Its girth six feet from the ground is thirty-two feet! I think it might be called Big Tom."

It developed that Big Tom was also an inveterate bee hunter and collector of spruce gum. "As we approached the top, Big Tom pointed out the direction, a half-mile away, of a small pond, a little mountain tarn, overlooked by a ledge of rock, where Professor Mitchell lost his life. That day as we sat on the summit he gave in great detail the story, the general outline of which is well known."

Warner was much impressed by the story of the final burial of Mitchell on the summit of the mountain that bears his name, after the hardy mountain people had hacked their way through the wilderness for three days en route with his body. "Such a strange cortège had never before broken the silence of this lonely wilderness, nor was ever burial more impressive than this wild interment above the clouds. . . . The mountain is his monument. . . . It is the most majestic, the most lonesome grave on earth."

When the party had descended the mountain a little distance, they stopped for lunch under a threatening sky. Warner notes, "Our lunch was eaten in haste. Big Tom refused the chicken he had provided for us, and strengthened himself with slices of raw salt pork, which he cut from a hunk with his clasp-knife." Eventually, after a sharp encounter with a thunder storm, the men arrived at the widow Patten's on the far side of the mountain, horses and men completely fagged after scrambling and slipping about over twelve miles of Mount Mitchell country—all but Big Tom, who was still fresh and talking as usual.*

*I have used "The History of the Toe River Valley to 1865" by Jason Deyton (unpublished M.A. thesis, University of North Carolina) as a source of historical data in sketching the picture of the early days in Yancey County and the War period in the Valley.

IV

Guerillas

The flare of interest in the natural beauty of the Toe Valley excited by the Clingman-Mitchell interlude was shortly snuffed out as men began to argue slavery and secession whenever they met at the court house, the church, or a chicken fight. The Negro question made no great difference to the Valley, with only three hundred and sixty-two slaves in the whole district and most of those in the southern part. The Penlands were about the only slaveholding family north of the river. The Rock Creek section between Bakersville and the Roan had no Negroes at all, and has none today, because colored people have a well-founded belief that if they venture up there they might not come back alive. The southern part of the county was generally in favor of the Secession Convention and the northern part opposed. The vote finally went against the convention 576–548.

As soon as war was declared, the Valley split in two. The northern half, which supported the Union, wanted to part company with the Secessionist southern half. They succeeded in bringing about the separation in 1861 and named their new county, which was formed out of pieces subtracted from Watauga, Caldwell, Burke, and Yancey counties, after Professor Elisha

Uncle Zack McHone remembers the war time well in these dragging days when he can do nothing but lean against the headboard of his bed and clean out his pipe now and then

Mitchell. Calhoun, on the bottom land where Toe River skirts Humpback Mountain, not far from Samuel Bright's old place, became the county seat.

The heads of families, loving a good fight, and brought up on the tradition of King's Mountain, hurried out of the Valley to join Federal or Confederate forces at the nearest recruiting station. There was a small group in the southwestern part of the district who were unwilling to fight for either side, but they were no great asset to the women and children left behind by the soldiers. The wave of patriotic enthusiasm that carried the best men out of the Valley to one army or the other had a disillusioning backwash when impossible taxes were levied. By one decree the tax rate in Yancey County jumped to 150 percent of the amount levied at the beginning of the year—from $1.90 to $4.65. The property of Confederate soldiers was exempted and the Union families complained bitterly. People accustomed to paying their road tax in labor and everything else by barter could not meet the demands for taxes to be paid in cash. Even the most ardent Confederate families cooled off a little.

As if things were not bad enough, certain staples failed entirely. There was no salt. The government appointed an official agent to direct salt importation from Virginia and distribute it to Confederate families at ten cents a pound for hauling. It was a gesture in the right direction, but it did not work. For some reason the office of salt agent in Yancey County was declared vacant three times in a single year. Smallpox broke out, and the distracted county government established pest houses at Pensacola. There was an epidemic of lawlessness as the mountains became a refuge for deserters and malcontents who preyed upon the women and children. By December, 1862, conditions had become so desperate that the Yancey County court declared that not another man could be spared with the Valley families living in constant danger of pillage. In Mitchell County Confederate sympathizers were most likely to be mistreated; in Yancey, the families of Union men. Mont Ray, who had come home without leave from the Confederate army, and formed a lawless band of his own numbering a hundred men, captured the court house at Burnsville and broke up the recruiting station established to round up deserters.

By the spring of 1864 a Home Guard, made up of Confederate sympathizers above the age of conscription, was formed to punish the guerillas and catch the deserters. A war-within-a-war developed which instead of relieving the defenseless families increased their suffering.

Doc Hoppas, the son of a Union soldier, says, "It makes me mad to even think of the Home Guard for the way they done my daddy and my grand-mammy. When the war come, they drove off all the men into one army or the other, and then after a while they said they had to have a Home Guard to take care of the women and children. Hit was a militia they raised up, but they didn't take care of 'em. They tuck *from* 'em. They was the hatefullest, thievin' bunch there was. Down at Jim Bailey's they come in and found a little cloth in the loom Aunt Polly was weavin' to make John some clothes and they cut it out and took it with 'em. If a family hadn't a thing to depend on but their cow's milk, they'd kill her for beef right in the yard and leave 'em with nothin'.

"My daddy was Allison Hoppas that was son of Ebe Hoppas that's buried with Yankee soldiers at Knoxville. His pappy was Adam Hoppas that come from across the water in Ireland. When he come in this country he married Old Link's daughter and heir-ed all the Grassy Creek land from him, but he lost it again puttin' up money on slaves.

"My grandmammy seen hard times after grandpap went with the Union.

In the mountains there is always time to go hunting

There is something to be said for small houses, and farming that requires only part of the day

She was a Buchanan, sister to Lewis Buchanan that was my wife's grandpap. This here militia knowed grandpap was with the Union but they suspicioned he was home layin' out. One day they come and got grandma and said they'd make her tell where he was so they could get him. She told them the truth— all she knowed. He was gone to the War and she hadn't seen him no more'n they had. They wouldn't believe her and kept at her until finally they dragged her out to the fence and lifted up the top rail where it sets, alternating one on top of the other at the joints, and put her fingers in between and walked on the rails. They thought then she'd have to tell, but she couldn't tell what she didn't know. When she was give out and they got tired of that, they picked on my daddy that was just a little boy. He had a great big pet dog and they figured he'd tell anything to keep 'em from hurting his dog. Of course he couldn't tell neither. Then they said if he wouldn't they'd make him chop up his dog with the axe. And that's what they done. He had to hack him to pieces on the door stone to the house. When I heard him tell that when I was growin' up, I turned Republican right then, and I been so ever since. Two of us children was Democrats and two Republicans, so we just killed each other's votes regular, come election."

Uncle Rube Mosley did not get into the war between the states because he was only ten years old when Sumter was fired upon, but he remembers that "hit was awful for the folks in the mountains which ever army came through. They stripped the beds, cleaned anything they wanted out of the houses, robbed the bee gums and the hen roosts, lugged off the corn out of the cribs, and drove off the cattle and hogs, and of course they took the horses. Anything that could travel."

Uncle Zack McHone remembers the war time well in these dragging days when he can do nothing but lean against the headboard of his bed and clean out his pipe now and then. The thoughts of those days worry him.

"When the war come, I felt awful southern, and I went in Johnson's army of the West," he says, pulling down the old cap he wears in bed to foil the drafts that edge in the cracks in the wall. "I don't know how many battles I was in. We had 'em every day—big ones and little ones, and always goin' somewheres else. I recollect Chickamauga, though, and Powder Springs and New Hope Church. You just look at that bayonet. I been in lots of fights where we used 'em. You'd think they'd pull out easy when you've stuck a man. No sir. You've got to set your knee agin 'em and pull hard. No, they won't come out easy.

"Then I guarded at Andersonville. I just lie here lots of days thinking about how I'd go in the prison pens to gather up the dead. They didn't feed 'em, so they starved if they couldn't get no pick-ups. They was glad to eat meal bran if they could get it. But the Yankees had prisons and I suppose they treated our men bad too, so hit was fair. I felt sorry for 'em, though. I was lucky and never was wounded or captured the whole time of the war. Then I came home to Mitchell County in April, 1865. So I missed Kirk's maraudin' robber band."

Colonel George W. Kirk of the Third North Carolina U.S. Volunteers (organized at Knoxville), who drew many Confederate deserters into his regiment, is either a hero or a rascal according to which side is talking about him. The old factional tradition still holds on Toe River. For a time Kirk's admirers gained control of Mitchell County, and much plundering was done in his name whether he sanctioned it or not.

During the war Isaac English was living over near the Yellow Mountain. As a child he had been shot through the shoulder and was disabled for active service. Although Union in sympathy, he had been drafted by the Confederate government into civilian service to work in the iron mines at Cranberry.

*If a man needs extra help, he calls in his neighbors, and repays the service
when they call on him*

One night a man named McFall brought four Yankee officers across the ridge from McDowell County and handed them over to English. They had tunnelled their way out of a prison camp in Columbia, South Carolina, and worked their way northward. About one o'clock one morning the four men walked through the village of Marion and disappeared into the mountains. A Union sympathizer, Harvey Greenlee, found them and got an old Negro woman to feed them. The old woman gave them food, but she wanted to feel Colonel Gere's head to see if he had horns. She had been told the Yankees had them.

Greenlee turned them over to McFall, and he brought them to Isaac English, who was to try to get them to Kirk's army at the Winding Stairs near Linville. English knew the risk he was taking in aiding the enemy, but he was willing to stand by his convictions. He hid the men in a rock cave and brought them food as often as he could. If any one accosted him on his trips to the men, he explained that he was out to "gentle his hogs." The food was well concealed under corn in a split basket. After two weeks the time seemed auspicious to risk running the fugitives through to the Union lines. The entire trip to Linville and return over the mountains in the dark must be made before early morning, when he had to appear at Cranberry at the government works, and there was an excellent chance that they would none of them reach the lines.

As soon as it was dark enough, the men came down the mountain and into the lean-to kitchen of the English log house. Alice Jane, English's wife, had a big meal waiting for them, but just as they started to eat, a man hallooed outside. The four soldiers dived under the beds where the long flounces hid them. Mrs. English put the tell-tale plates out of the way and Isaac opened the door.

It was a neighbor who wanted to borrow fire, but he also wanted to talk, and every minute spent before English and the fugitives could set out on the journey cut down their chances of getting through the lines. At last the neighbor went away. English kissed his wife and the five men started on the dash over the ridges. Morning saw English back at his post and the Yankees safe in the Union army. The cave on the banks of Toe River where he hid the northern officers is still called the Yankee Rocks.

Peace came to the Toe River country, not with the surrender at Appomattox, but draggingly, like a swing slowing to a stop. The mountain people had many private grudges to be settled; they could not cease fighting among themselves just because two distant generals had agreed to stop. The Valley was in the midst of the isolation period that had begun imperceptibly to close down on the hill country when the last great migration passed westward in 1850.

V

Chaos and Isolation

The state government at Raleigh had enough trouble with its wretched Negro rule without worrying about the hill country on the farthest bounds of the state. If affairs were bad up there, the mountain people must work out their own solution. The years spent in doing it have welded them into a race fiercely individualistic and distrustful of outside influences. Their problems were different from those of the lowlands and they intended to keep them different.

For a long time the mountain people had been unconsciously drawing together, thinking of themselves as a separate entity; if in effect this indicated a growing isolation, they welcomed it. The convenient mountain barriers meant that they ran their own country in their own way with little interference from the distant state government. The isolation of the mountains following the war was as much the proud withdrawal of the hill people into themselves and the stubborn conservatism of opinion at variance with the low country as it was geographical.

Without difficulty the hill people disposed of the Negro problem that harassed the low country. Negroes were few in the hills; if more came, they were driven out. It was harder to break up the guerilla bands that were

To Uncle Rube Mosley the past is only day before yesterday

ravaging the Valley. It had never been easy to keep order in the mountains. Now, as the country emerged from the license of war, it got out of control.

Uncle Rube Mosley, his long frame overflowing the curvebacked mountain-made chair in lean angles, his pointed keen face accentuated by the triangular beard that makes him look like one of the disciples, remembers that he had a good time in Kirk's Army, helping to put the state in order. He "kivered all the ground he stood on" and he "could fight like a fair hellion."

"I got growed in time to join up in Kirk's Army," he says, "and I seen service puttin' down the Ku Klux. We stopped 'em too, but now really they was good people. They was lied on and misrepresented. I hadn't no fault to find with them, but hit don't seem like they ought to killed Senator Stevens like they did.

"That was in Alamance County.* We took a hundred and thirteen of 'em in the court house after that and we got the man that killed him. Sheriff Wiley was his name, and he was caught by Bill Birchfield, Nathan Birchfield, and Bill H. O'Brien. After they got him, he was penned in the very room where Senator Stevens' blood was splashed all over the wall, and he was the uneasiest man ever I seen. Three or four days he just walked all the time. They put him in with all the blood marks a-purpose, so he could be thinkin' on what he done. I don't know what happened to him. I remember though there was a nigger hung while we was located there. A nigger called Andy. I don't know what he was hung for, but I recollect that Uncle Jackson Campbell preached his funeral sermon before they hung him.

"When we was coming back, they sent flat cars for us to Salisbury and we was all boozed up and mean as snakes. That was because they had bushwhacked us the night before. I didn't figure we was going to get rations on that flat-car, so when I come aboard I had me a half-gallon jar of oysters under my arm. I ate 'em that night and gave out some to my friends. The train just dragged along slow like a wagon and when we run through a cut there was the Ku Klux Klan lined up either side waitin' for us and we havin' to run between 'em and get it both sides. I got five bullet holes in my knapsack when I was squattin' down, trying to keep low, but they never touched me. I was lucky.

*William B. Williamson of Asheville, whose father was familiar with the details of the case, says that the Stevens murder occurred in Caswell County and that the murderer was never found. Apparently Uncle Rube has confused parts of two different murders, one in Alamance County and one in Caswell.

A path of rocks slopes down to Bird Ellis' spring house

"That day I done one of the meanest things in my life. I sat hit was mean because hit was unprovoked. We was ridin' along slow, like I said, and we passed close to an old man diggin' potatoes in a field. As we come by he never looked up nor raised his head. That made me mad. I like to have folks speak to me. When I see a man, I give him a greeting or at least show that I seen him if he is a stranger or not. So I picked up that empty half gallon oyster jar that was kickin' around under foot and threw it at him. Hit took him on the back of his head close under his neck. I seen him drop forward like a stone. We'd been puttin' his country in order. He ought to have looked up at us anyhow.

"Once I hired out to three Rebels. These was Georgia Rebels and hit was after I left Cloudland and started working on the C.C. & O. I was goin' to work a gang for 'em and we agreed on $1.20 a day. They was to pay us once a month, on the twentieth, and I had that day all fixed in my mind so I'd know when it came and lay off. I never figured to work on pay day.

"Well, the twentieth come and in the morning me and the men was all standing around top of the cut waitin' for our money when Captain Jo Howell come up to us and says,

"'What you doin' up there? Why ain't you in the cut workin'?'

"'I don't aim to work on pay day,' I says, 'and this is the twentieth when you agreed to pay off.'

"Then he began beating around the bush and sayin' he had said he would pay the Saturday *following* the twentieth—which he hadn't.

"'All right then, let's hang him, boys,' I says to my men. 'If he won't pay us when he says, we'll get that much satisfaction!' So we took him in custody. He begged off until night, swearin' he didn't have the money, and I guess maybe he didn't. We kept him where he wouldn't run off though, and he promised to give us store orders on Shay MacDonald, that was one of the bloodthirstiest buggers that ever lived. Captain Howell told me if I'd take the orders to MacDonald, instead of my getting $1.20 for the day, he'd give me two dollars.

"'Done,' I says, knowing MacDonald couldn't eat me.

"When I went to MacDonald he wouldn't give me nothin' on the orders (and I hadn't much thought he would). 'All right,' I told him, 'keep your money and we'll just hang the Captain. We got him in custody where he won't get loose.'

"'Don't do that!' he yells. 'I'll send a man to pay off as soon as I can get the money.'

"'We'll wait till three o'clock and no later,' I promised, and lit out for camp. I really expected they would send a man to pay off after that, but I thought hit wouldn't hurt to have a little fun with the Captain. So when I got back I didn't say that MacDonald had promised to send the money. I just told how he wouldn't honor the orders and directed the boys to put a rope on Captain Howell. He was being kept in a tobacco barn, and right near was a high gate which was just the thing if we did need to hang him.

"I says, 'Leave him walk around and talk a spell first.'

"I had the men put the rope around his waist and let him travel up and down the road in front of the high gate. Then hit kept gettin' on toward the time I'd set with MacDonald and I didn't like this paradin' around so long.

"All at once I seen a nigger come runnin' head-long. I trained my gun on him and told him to stop. He did, you bet, scart of his life, and he had been sent by Shay to say they was bringing the money fast as they could.

"We got paid directly and let Captain Howell go. I got my two dollars he promised for that day, too. I always aimed to arrest him sometime on some kind of a charge just to show him I could do it, but I got called somewhere else to work before I got the chance. I was deputized by the government for eighteen years to arrest people."

At the first session of the Superior Court in Mitchell County after the war, thirty people were indicted for robbery. All but two of the cases tried that term were for larceny or assault. Court continued to be held at Calhoun until 1866, when Judge J. W. Bowman of Bakersville, representative of the district in the state legislature, introduced a measure allowing the people to vote on where the capital should be located. The people in the western part of the county, Bowman's home, carried the election. Today, all there is left of the once honored Calhoun is a flat field and a wallow of blackberries and laurel. Not even a rotting log marks the site of the old court house.

The court was moved before there was a building to hold it. It sat under the shade of a grove of trees near the site of the present court house until a log building was raised for the purpose. If the setting was primitive, not so the judges. They had an audience drawn from forty miles around, many of whom had come all of the way on foot. The crowds milled up and down the streets day and night, especially nights. The judges dressed in top hats and

Across the road is a field of corn shocks

long-tailed coats for each grand promenade from the hotel to the bench, attended by the sheriff to escort His Honor in style. "Make way for His Honor! Clear the way!" and the judge marching behind with never a glance to the side.

Doc Hoppas of Brushy Creek tells the story of an episode during court week that belongs to the period after Bakersville became the county seat, when the first rancour of the war years had begun to die out.

COURT WEEK

If you're not on the docket, court week is a treat,
When the folks go up to the county seat.
They used to get rough. One time was a sight.
They carried on high. Ye'd think that they might
A known the Judge wouldn't stand for that,
And the third day mornin' he come out flat.
"No liquor!" he says. "Ye disgrace the court!
There's a law against corn. Chief Thompson, report
To me any man that you find with a drink.

Burge Bailey built a stout pole barn, roofed with shakes,
above the dam at Penland

He'll go to the chain-gang for long as I think
Will make the rest of you all think twice
Before doin' the same." And he meant it. The price
Of corn went up. A fellow down town
Got caught with some and the Judge sent him down
On the county road like he said he would.
Then the town sobered up. Not even Zack could
Get hold of a drop of corn anywhere
And he could have got whatever was there.
Zack Stone and Deal Ransom would never go dry.
They had to have somethin' and someone said, "Try
A bottle of tonic. Hit's part alcohol."
They bought some Cheruna. I guess they got all
The store keeper had before they was through.
Of course there was other ones drinkin' it too.
And then they drunk Syrup of Indian Weed.
There was plenty in stock, all they would need.
They liked it right well. Things waked up a bit.

The Judge was right sharp though. He got onter it
And said no more of the stuff could be sold
Without a prescription. Ye'd think that would hold
Zack and Deal for a while. But they got holt of Paul,
The son of the doctor, and he wrote 'em all
The prescriptions they wanted. (Paul's off in the head
And he thought he had to do just what they said.)
He writes mighty well. Hit's the most he can do.
They got permits enough to last 'em clear through
Till the Judge went away. But he found what they'd done,
(The Doc missed the blanks) and so every one
That come fur prescriptions was let in fur trouble.
He aimed to collect and make 'em pay double,
And then I'll tell you, the town was dead.
Zack and Deal sulled up. That night instead
Of hangin' around with the rest of the men
They was mad as hornets and scowled you down when
Ye as much as looked at 'em. They just went walkin',
Glowerin' and sulky and neither one talkin'.
They ran on Coy Torbett. He pulled his coat back
And winked and says sly-like, "Look a here, Zack!
See what I found that someone had hid
By the steps at the Hotel. All that I did
Was look out of the window and there was the shine
Of the light on the glass!" "That air stuff is mine!"
Says Zack to him, talkin' rough like he's mad,
"Were ye aimin' to take the last corn I had?
Give it here!" He snatched it. "Now next time you see
My corn by the steps, ye just leave it be.
Of course I know you didn't intend
To grab off a bottle of corn from a friend—"
Zack did it like that. Coy argued some
But they carried it off and then they come
Up to the court house and eased in behind
To try it out. Says Deal, "Is your mind
Quite easy, Zack, about that quart?
Hit seems to me that any sort

Of feller whose corn we'd want to drink
Would be too cautious to ever think
He could leave a bottle right in sight
With the town as dry as it is tonight."
"I'd studied some about that too.
We need it awful. What'll we do?"
"Why don't you have a snort and see
How good that corn appears to be?"
"I'd rather not. Suppose I tried
To sample it, and then I died!"
Said Deal, "We'd better, if we can,
Experiment on another man."
And Zack suggested, "Just suppose
We looked around right smart and chose
A man we wouldn't mind to lose.
There's two or three I'd like to choose."
"Kaint do no hurt, Zack," Deal agreed.
"We'll pick a man don't no one need.
Suppose he dies! We're doin' good,
Let's start right off. I think we should."
"Watch out," Zack warned. "Let's not spare much.
I'm awful dry, but we won't touch
A drop of it until we know.
I met a man a while ago
I'd like to give some. Let's get goin'.
Hit seems a sight of fuss fur knowin'
If we can drink this corn or not."
"There's Rankin comin', I'd forgot
His being here. He's done some killin'.
How'll he do?" "No. He's distillin'.
I'd hate to cut down the supply.
Hit's low enough, Deal. He goes by."
They greeted Rankin and passed on.
"I'm wonderin' where McQuade has gone.
There ain't a thing he wouldn't steal
And he won't work. He suit ye, Deal?"
"He's a sorry un, but let's begin

The corn crib at Deer Park stands by the sheep meadow where John Bailey built his first cabin

On someone else. McQuade's my kin.
There's Sanford comin'. He's our man!
I know he's done more mean things than
A low-down triflin' nigger'd do—"
"Hold on there, Deal! Suppose it's true.
There's plenty on the other side.
Haint his wife's kinfolks always tried
To meddle in? I'll grant he's bad
But you'd be worse if you had had
To live with her fur more'n a day."
"I wouldn't a picked her anyway.
That's his fault. . . . We've let two get by.
Hit seems to me, Zack, if you shy
Off every single man I get—"
"I haint shied off. We'll pick one yet.
Wa'nt you the one said 'Leave McQuade!'"
"Well, you said 'No' first choice I made!"
"I'll bet that corn is awful good.

Just taste it, Deal, I would you would."
"I wouldn't touch it, Zack, look there!
Columbus Carr's our man. See where
He's standing yander in the door
Of the boarding house. Let's ask afore
We waste more time. He's mean enough,
A regular stealin' spyin' tough.
What say? He bad enough fur you?"
"Hit's gettin' late, Deal. Yes, he'll do.
Corn's so scarce, just leave him taste it.
He's too worthless. We kaint waste it."
They greeted Carr. "Say, want to come
Along with us? We're drinkin' some."
Zack pulled his coat back. "Carr, look here!
Want some? Turn your back." "All clear?"
"Nobody lookin'. Go ahead!"
"Thank ye, boys, fur that," he said.
"Hit holped me out. Let's set a spell."
The three sat down. "Ye feelin' well?"
Asked Zack and dipped a bit of snuff.
"No. I ain't. I feel right tough."
Deal and Zack exchanged quick glances.
Zack said, "Well, I take no chances.
Watch out what ye eat and drink."
And Carr says to him, "Sure, I think
A feller ought to take some care.
How much corn ye got to spare?"
"Be careful, Carr! That's powerful stuff."
"Hit's fine; I'd never get enough."
"Well, hit's your funeral. Go ahead.
Have another," Ransom said.
Columbus did. He took a lot.
"Zack," he says, "I'm gettin' hot.
What d'ye say? Let's take a walk."
Carr felt lively, full of talk.
"When you fellers came along
I wasn't feelin' awful strong.

The last two days I've had a cold,
And needed whiskey. I can hold
A sight of corn. Hit's right smart good.
I'm feeling fine." "I'd think you would!"
Zack looked cross. "Ye sunk it some."
He turned to Deal. "He better come
Along home now. Let's get him back.
I see Old Thompson's on his track."
Deal gave a comprehending wink.
"Yes. I saw him. Do you think
He'll make us trouble? Carr, keep quiet!"
"I'm feared he will. He's goin' to try it."
"Zack, we're goin' to see him through!"
"Hold on! What you all tryin' to do?"
Carr looked at Zack and Deal in doubt.
"Are you two fellers makin' out
Two drinks of corn would make me high?
Sure I seen the Chief go by.
He never gave a look at me."
"Oh yes, he did. (He didn't see
How Thompson had his eye on him.
He's bad off, Deal! Full to the brim.
We've got to get him off the street.
Don't he know hit's the County Seat?)"
Columbus begged, "Now I ain't ready
To go home yet. I'm just as steady—"
"You *think* you are. I say you ain't.
You've reached the point now where you kaint
Remember half what you been doin'.
You've got the pair of us a stewin'
For fear that we'll be pulled in too
Fur bein' caught along with you.
You better come and leave us pack
You safe in bed. We'll take you back.
The things we've seen you do tonight!
The Chief'll jail ye just for spite."
"I'm a peaceable man. You boys kin swear

"Uncle Tom Sparks built a sash sawmill over near Lockridge's place"

I ain't done nothing anywhere."
"You tried to pick a fight with Deal
That's your good friend! And he don't feel
To stand too much. And at the store
You got so wild, we thought before
We got you out you'd wreck the place."
"I'm high all right if that's the case.
I guess that's what I'm like to do
When I'm just right. Boys, see me through!
Get me to bed." "We're aimin' to."
They took him home. He'd taken more
Than they had planned to spare before.
"Hit cost too much to try it out,"
Says Zack when Carr was gone. "I doubt
His needin' much that second one."
And then Deal says, "Leave go what's done.
Count out that couple of drinks of his.
We've got the only corn there is!"

Over on the Deer Park lands James Bailey was starting two innovations. He founded the first game preserve in western North Carolina and he erected the first local sash sawmill. One day he had a chance to get two fawns from a man named Robinson. His wife raised them with great care, because they were extremely delicate, feeding them boiled milk until they could eat other food. In 1875 Bailey posted his land in order to protect the fawns. The refuge he maintained for two animals could as well shelter others, so he added to his herd. In time there were a hundred deer on the slope below the house. By 1878 he set aside fifty acres for them and bounded it with a tall stake-and-rider fence, but it took more than the fence to insure safety.

When the land was first closed to hunters, the mountain people flatly refused to believe that there was such a thing as the Posting Law. They ignored the Park boundaries, came over the fence, ran the deer with dogs, and killed them. The family was warned against trying to maintain the game refuge in the face of public opinion. Even when trespassers were punished and the fact was established that the state would uphold the posting of land, hunters ignored the restriction and kept on killing the deer. The animals had

The English Inn, like an old sailing ship washed up on the bank in a cove

been hunted practically to extinction on the neighboring hills. The fine deer herd was too tempting.

In the face of repeated reprisals upon their personal property, the Baileys stoutly maintained the sanctity of the deer refuge. Petty acts of ill will continually harassed them. Pet dogs were poisoned; crops were damaged. Then their sawmill on the river was torn up, the sash saw damaged, and the tools thrown in the water. The Baileys accepted their loss and defended the Park as before, even in spite of threats to burn their buildings. People hesitated, however, to go that far for fear of running on to the sons, John or Pinck or Burge or Wes, who had a way of being in several parts of the estate at once. Sometimes a couple of them took quilts and slept in the barn to insure its safety.

One Christmas night three men came into the Park expecting to kill some of the tame deer easily. But at the approach of strangers the herd that came galloping at Aunt Polly's call vanished into the thickets like mist. Unable to find game, the trespassers tore down some twenty panels of the Park fence, thinking to let the whole herd loose where it could be hunted. Then going to the log barn beyond the house, they shot down a milch cow in the stable, left her where she lay, and fled in the dark.

The brothers heard the shot, discovered the cow in the stable, and started in pursuit. In the narrow bottom by the River they found where the marauders had left their horses. A tell-tale sack with the name of the store from which it had been bought furnished a partial clew. The boy who had held the horses while the men entered the Park was apprehended, and confessed. Thus the identity of the trespassers was established. Two of them fled the country, but the third, the man who had done the shooting, was arrested and sent to the penitentiary. Warrants were kept renewed for the other two, who eventually returned, threw themselves on the mercy of the court, and paid for the damage.

There was one killing in the Park lands that the Baileys never forgave. A tame doe named Little Nan had been sent for safe-keeping to the Deer Park from Marion, North Carolina. She promptly attached herself to the family instead of to the deer herd and haunted the door steps, begging for attention. One day young Wesley Bailey came into the kitchen to find her curled up on the cot bed in the corner. Eventually Nan became such a nuisance that she had to be exiled to the paddock, but instead of joining the other deer, she persisted in trotting up and down the fence looking mournfully into the yard. Then one day as she grazed quietly with her fawn, a trespasser shot and killed her.

Gradually the feeling about the Deer Preserve changed. It became an institution of local pride. People came from far and near to see the animals. Hardly a week passed when there were less than six or eight guests at the Bailey home and there was need of the big bedrooms and many beds. No penny was ever taken for the entertainment of these visitors.

The sash sawmill that James Bailey built in 1872 was practically a crank whip-saw which ran up and down in a frame, using water power from a wheel set horizontally instead of the usual overshot vertical type. Some of the first timber sawed was intended for additions to the Deer Park house. It burned up in the dry kiln. James and his sons cut and sawed more logs, built a second story on the house, and clapboarded it. In 1880 they put a dam across the river to provide power for a second mill. The logs were fastened with locust pins, calculated to stand strain. James was sick, but he could not keep away from the river where his sons were carrying on the work. He used up the last of his strength stubbornly hewing locust pins, until he died on the first day of the New Year.

Doc Hoppas, who lives up the Hollow above the first Bailey mill, likes to talk about the lumber business in the old days, as he sits on the porch of a Sunday afternoon cooling off from the hot walk up the hill to church at Estatoe and back.

"About the time Jim Bailey started his mill there begun to be several mills all at once," he says. "They had to have something to grind corn and they got rigged to cut timber too. There was little notches in the sash saw machine to feed the log along, whether you stayed and watched it or not, and if it finished while you weren't looking, it made no difference. Uncle Tom Sparks built a sash sawmill over near Lockridge's place and Lewis Buchanan had one. He got killed in his, one Sunday, when he went over to grind a little run of meal for dinner, and got caught by his shirt. There wa'n't nobody there to turn him loose so he was whipped to pieces.

"We done all our chopping, of course, with axes, and squared off the ends with the axe, too. There wa'n't any cross-cut saws yet. Plenty of lumber that went out of here by ox team to Marion and Cranberry was whip-sawed. That was real work. We'd pick a sidling bank and roll logs out on skid-poles laid from the top of the bank into the crotch of a tree lower down. That would leave a place for the man sawing on the bottom side to get in under. He and the man on the upside each hewed to a line and it worked very well.

"I recollect when the first cross-cut saw come in the country. Jimmy Bailey and Josh Bailey, Tom Sparks and Lewis Buchanan, all went together and were partners in a cross-cut saw that they had sent away for. Hit hadn't no drag teeth but it cut even. When they got it, each one was so afraid the other would do something to spoil it they never let just one use it alone. They wythed it on a board for fear it would take hurt if it bent, and then when they got it set to cut they'd ease the board away. They had themselves a time when it needed to be sharpened. It took the hull of 'em to do that. They were so choice of that saw, it would be here yet if it hadn't burnt up. Hit was just a curiosity, though. They only used it for house timber and such as that. In the woods we used axes right on and the women were stout enough to step up and take their turn. We none of us cared for work. My wife has packed plenty of wood out of steep places on her back and so have I.

"Finally, Clem Ellis, that's Ed Ellis' father, and Rube Woody brought in

The North Toe River dodges through the laurel and rhododendron of the high wooded valley to join the South Toe near Toecane and form the Nolichucky

the first circle-saw we ever seen and set hit up on Brushy Creek. That was in 1893 when I was ten years old. Hit run by steam and folks were afraid of it but they came for miles and miles and stayed all day and brought their dinner just to see it run. John Silvers got the second circle-saw. All the timber was still going out to Marion and Cranberry with ox teams, six and eight head to a wagon, but they couldn't haul much even then, not with a axle draggin' in the mud. Those days were hard on everybody—oxen and mules and folks.

"After my Daddy forsook Ma and us children, she didn't have nothing and we got nothing to eat only as we went after it and made it. The neighbors tried to get her to give us away but she stayed with us right on. There wa'n't no jobs to get to speak of. If you got fifty cents a day you were flyin'. We lived near the Thompson Barrens on the Long Branch, close to Crabtree. Sometimes Ma could get a day's work for us over to Spruce Pine at $.50 for the hull of us. That was $.25 for her and 12½¢ for me and my brother. I was about 12 and him 14. We were tough and could hoe as good as she could, but that was the wages. We'd walk from our place to where we was working and be in the field till night. Then we'd go to Berry's store by English's Inn

This is a country-within-a-country, ringed with mountain barriers—an outpost with customs of its own in a country with different folk-ways

and get us our provisions and pack 'em home. We'd have to shin over all the ridges back to Crabtree in the dark and I'll tell you hit was a snake country. You just had to take your chance of tromping on 'em and bear away from where you heard 'em sing. Hit would be midnight when we got home and no fire nor light. All there was to do was crawl in the bed in the dark and glad to get there. Ma'd always lift the top quilt off and give it a smart flirt before she let us get in, just in case a snake could a crawled in during the day while we were gone. You never know'd for sure if you might be gettin' in to bed with one in the dark. I was young and rested directly, but Ma would be whipped down. Come morning I'd have to go over a mile for fire and then we'd work our own land.

"Ma rented a piece that had been planted to corn the year before. This was the second year for it. We hadn't no way to plow it, of course, not having no animals, but we made us a crop. I went ahead of Ma and pulled up the stalks left standing from last year and she came along and dropped the corn in the hole, and my brother behind her stomped it down. If I come to a hill where the stalk had failed last year, it was my job to dig out a hole with my toes or my fingers. We made a hundred bushels of corn that year and then we were fixed to feed ourselves and a pig.

"We put the piece to wheat next and dug it with hoes. Hit was awful to save our stuff from the wild turkeys. The country was full of them. Sometimes I've seen eighteen at a time in our lot and we hadn't no gun nor powder. Quick as you went for 'em they'd rise, but when you left, back they came.

"John McBee's daddy sent for Ma to come down after awhile and he give her a brood sow and ten pigs to keep for him. We got half the litter for tending 'em. The most you had to do was to keep an eye on 'em, because they'd pick a living in the woods. They just multiplied and multiplied until the brush was full of them. Ma sent him word to come get his half but he never did, so when we moved off'n that place we left his. They was perfectly wild, running everywhere.

"Ma kept figuring a little here and there and she raised us even if we never had nothing laid by. When I married we had nothing either, but we raised our children. They're gone by themselves now, and the worst we got to put up with is being lonesome."

CHAPTER

VI

Cloudland

In the '70's gentlemen armed with plate cameras and young ladies of fashion in bustles and flounces from the world beyond the mountains began to ride up Roan Mountain on the boundary between Tennessee and North Carolina to patronize Colonel John Wilder's Cloudland Hotel. Roan Mountain, 6313 feet high, is magnificently imposing as the crowning height of the Iron Mountains, and yet accessible from both sides by way of Carver's Gap. There was a hack line built up the mountain from Little Rock Creek in 1873 and another from Magnetic City in '75. Uncle Rube Mosley helped build six miles of road from Tennessee.

"I was always used to workin' a gang of men and I could handle 'em," he says. "Agin the hotel opening, General John Wilder, that owned most all the land, gave me a bunch of hands to build a good six miles of hack line from Burbank. I holp build that road and fell the timber too, to build the Cloudland Hotel that set atop the mountain. I stayed up there ten years in all.

"When the road was done I stayed around and cut spruce logs. Hit was too thickety to afford to use a saw. We had axes. By Christmas that year we had 100,000 foot of lumber on the stick. I was a strong man in those days.

Many's a time I've said, 'Let's holp the teamsters out, boys,' when we'd be going in for dinner, and then picked up a ten-foot log and walked off with it.

"Nights I'd lie in the camp bed hearin' the wolves howl. I never knew of more'n one or two bears on the Roan, but there was plenty over across on Big Yellow and on Humpback. We pretty well broke up the wolf pack. Hit was the little blue ones. I recollect Uncle Ad Buchanan runnin' on a den about a mile north of the camp. He killed the old dog on the spot and took five puppies alive. The female wasn't there, but we got her close to the road on the Tennessee side. I took one of the puppies down to Roan Mountain Station and sold it to Huse Merridy. He kept it three years tied to his front gate. Days hit was gentle, but nights you didn't want to trifle with it. They learnt it that way for a watch-dog. Dave Correl got another one of 'em and I've seen hit nurse his wife's breast. Hit grew up as gentle as you could ask. Sometimes we'd fish in a cove with our hands, in a good place we knew, where water backed up to a big rock and there was lots of fish. That little wolf would stand on the bank lookin' so hopeful we'd throw him one every now and then and you ought to see him catch 'em in his mouth."

In these days before automobiles when travellers climbed the Roan, they were prepared to stay long enough to repay them for their trouble. By 1879 a tri-weekly hack ran regularly from the Eastern Tennessee-Virginia and Georgia Railroad to the Cloudland Hotel. People who spent several weeks in the solitudes of the great bald with nothing else to do but scramble up and down the coves and marvel at the view, came to know and love every inch of the mountain. Someone was always discovering a new wonder.

A newspaper of 1878 describes a glen on the mountain from which issued an eery humming music. The account of the phenomenon is written by Henry E. Colton, of Knoxville, Tennessee, under the heading Scientific News.

"Several of the cattle tenders on the mountain and also General Wilder had spoken to us about what they called Mountain Music. One evening they said it was sounding loud, and Dr. D. P. Boynton, of Knoxville, Hon. J. M. Thornburg, and myself accompanied General Wilder to the glen to hear it. The sound was very plain to the ear, and was not at all as described—like the humming of thousands of bees—but like the incessant, continuous and combined snap of two Leyden jars positively and negatively charged. I tried to account for it on the theory of bees or flies but the mountain people said it

A hack line was built up Little Rock Creek to Roan Mountain in 1873

frequently occurred after the bees or flies had gone to their winter homes or before they came out. It was always loudest and most prolonged just before there would be a thunderstorm in either valley, or one passing over the mountain. I used every argument I could to persuade myself that it was simply a result of some common cause and to shake the faith of the country people in its mysterious origin but I only convinced myself that it was the result from two currents of air meeting each other in the suck between the two peaks where there was no obstruction of trees, one containing a greater, the other a less amount of electricity, or that the two currents coming together in the open plateau on the high elevation, by their friction and being of different temperatures, generated electricity. The 'mountain music' was simply the snapping caused by this friction and this generation of electricity. Many have noted the peculiar snapping hum to be observed in great auroral displays, particularly those of September, 1859 and February, 1872.

"As the amount of electricity in the air currents became equalized or surcharged, they, descending to the other side caused the thunder storm daily in the valleys near the mountain and sometimes immediately on the edge of

Uncle Stokes Penland was running the hack line up Roan Mountain when Asa Gray made his famous botanical tour

Mount Mitchell rears up on the sky line, loftiest of all

the timber surrounding the great bald top. The air currents of the Western North Carolina mountains and the East Tennessee valley form an aerial tide, ebbing and flowing. The heated air of the valley rises from nine in the morning until three or four in the afternoon, making a slight easterly wind up and over Roan Mountain. As night comes on the current turns back into the valley, almost invariably producing a very brisk gale by three or four o'clock in the morning which, in its turn, dies down to a calm by seven and commences to reverse by nine o'clock. This continual change of currents of air makes it an impossibility for any great malarial scourge to exist in the East Tennessee valley, especially its northeastern end."

The same year that Colton gave his report on the "mountain music," sufferers from hay fever discovered that on the Roan they were free from their discomfort. So many people went to the Roan in order to escape the annoyance of the disease that they became known as The Hay Fever Brigade.

Charles Dudley Warner made the ascent from the Tennessee side in 1885 on his horseback trip to Asheville. His notes report the Hotel as providing

The road leads down through laurel shade and up over windy hilltops

two comfortable rooms for office and sitting room with partitioned-off sleeping places in the loft, adding that while it set a good table, it rocked like a ship at sea when the wind blew. He found the place full of pleasant young ladies botanizing, busy with long walks to watch the far-famed splendor of the Roan sunrise or to search for natural wonders in the glens; occupying themselves in the afternoons with croquet and pressing flowers. The culmination of the day was the evening vigil on Sunset Bluff for the dramatic disappearance of the sun.

Uncle Stokes Penland, who keeps the Penland House at Linville Falls, was running the hack line and taking charge of the outdoor work around the house for General Wilder in the '80's when Asa Gray, Regent of the Smithsonian and foremost naturalist of his time, made his famous botanical tour of the mountains. It was through General Wilder that Gray engaged Uncle Stokes as a guide. From his nine years as a "revenue" he had a good practical knowledge of every nook and cranny of the mountains from Virginia to Georgia. There were seven in Gray's party. For twenty days Uncle Stokes guided them through the Unakas, the Iron Mountains, and the Linville country. At that time Asa Gray was about fifty and Uncle Stokes in his early thirties. Now, old Uncle Stokes is anxious to know each spring if the beautiful bell-shaped lily which Gray first discovered on the Roan is still growing where they first found it. Of recent years its luxuriant growth has overtopped the rhododendron.

Margaret Morley writes delightfully of her journey to the top of the Roan in the later days of the Hotel, before it burned.

"Near the top of Roan, which is over sixty-three hundred feet high, is Cloudland Hotel where one dines in North Carolina and sleeps in Tennessee, the hotel being cut in two by the state line.

"Roan Mountain has long been famous for two things, the circular rainbow sometimes seen from the summit, and the variety of wild flowers that grow on its slopes, it being reported that more species are found here than in any other one place on the continent. One not a botanist going up in the summer will be delighted with the luxuriance and variety of colors assumed by the bee-balm, blood-red prevailing, although some of the springs and damp hollows are painted about with lavender, blush rose, dark rose-red, pale honey-yellow or white bee-balm, and all of them, no matter what the color, are full of humming-birds. The botanies have no idea how many colors this charming plant assumes on the open slopes of the Roan. From these slopes one gets fine views of the surrounding mountains, views sometimes framed in rose-bay bushes, when your imagination paints a glowing picture of the scene when the rose-bay is in bloom.

"Near the summit you will notice the little houstonia with plumy saxifrage and pink oxalis everywhere in the mosslike growths that cover the rocks, and you will also notice, although you may not know how rare it is, the large buttercup-like flower with a geranium leaf, the *Geum grandiflorum*. If it is summer you will see the bright flowers of the lily named after Asa Gray, it having been first captured on the Roan, although it is abundant all through the mountains. And you will be sure to taste the little high-flavored strawberries hiding on the grassy ledges.

"There are a few spruce and fir trees, mountain ashes and alders scattered about near the top, but otherwise the Roan presents wide reaches of pasture lands where flocks and herds are grazing. . . ."*

Today a traveller would not recognize the site of the old Hotel on the mountain top unless it were pointed out to him, but if the visitors are more transient they are no less numerous. The Roan is the same, year after year. Despoiled of her timber now on this side, now on that, she is imperishable. The work of man on her steep sides is no more than the bleaching of the black shadow that rimmed the bald. As you round the point of rock at the top of the hill above Loafer's Glory, after Ledger is left behind, the Roan awaits you, high and serene, and always there is that catch of the breath and the fumbling for a word to express what cannot be expressed when the great blue mass towers before you into the sky.

*The Carolina Mountains. Courtesy of Houghton Mifflin Company.

CHAPTER

VII

Ground-Hog Holes

In 1858, the year following Professor Mitchell's death on Sugar Camp Creek, Thomas Clingman, newly appointed Democratic Senator from North Carolina, was back in the mountains again. He happened to stay overnight in the home of a Mr. Silvers near Bakersville, where he found a window filled with large panes cut from sheets of mica. The sight inspired immediate action in Senator Clingman, who coupled restless activity with sprightly curiosity in natural developments. He wanted to see where the clear isinglass came from. When he was shown the early diggings, he hired workmen and sunk a shaft. Magnificent blocks of mica and feldspar, glittering with pyrites, came to light. He was not interested in the mica, but there was a promise of silver in the spar that brought him back to Sink Hole in 1867, after the war. A western miner to whom he showed a sample of the ore predicted that the silver would run as high as three hundred dollars to the ton. It never actually produced more than three dollars a ton, although he sank shafts well below the old workings and tunneled industriously.

One day a man named Heap, connected with a Knoxville stove works, came by and carried home a block of the despised mica. He found a market for it, and sometime in the early seventies he returned with E. B. Clapp. The

*The log upright which Isaac English added to his inn became the mica house of
Gere and English*

two formed the pioneer firm of Heap and Clapp to operate the Sink Hole for
mica. The underground work eventually amounted to between two and three
thousand feet and the results were gratifying.

As the market increased, the firm leased wide tracts of mineral land and
found more and more mica. The Cloudland deposit, accidentally discovered
in 1870 by Thomas Green as he was digging ginseng, but heretofore considered only a curiosity, was opened by the owner, encouraged by the success of
Heap and Clapp. It produced $4000 in two months, after which it was
worked by Abernathy and Rorison, and then by Heap and Clapp. A single
mica crystal 8″ × 24″ in the first large rock found by Green sold for $67. If it
had not been weathered, it would have brought $250. Colonel Irby esti-
mated that up to 1896 the Cloudland Mine had produced a hundred thousand dollars' worth of mica.

Some of the mica from the Hawk Mine produced clear sheets 18″ × 20″.
By 1896 it had produced $75,000 worth of mica, and another Heap and
Clapp property, the Clarissa on Cane Creek, $175,000. Eventually Heap

The holes of the Emerald Mine are full of water, and give back no light

sold out to Clapp, whose estate is still one of the largest holders of mineral lands in the district.

The Department of the Interior bulletin No. 740 estimates that the bulk of 400,000 pounds of mica mined in North Carolina from 1868 to 1882 came from the Heap and Clapp properties, most of which sold at from $2 to $11 a pound. Whereas the output once came from a few large mines, now most of it comes from seventy-five to a hundred small operations which are carried on intermittently.

An article entitled "Our Switzerland," in a Knoxville newspaper of fifty-seven years ago, describes a visit to one of the Heap and Clapp properties, evidently Cloudland, from its location on Mount Pezzle.

"Bakersville, Sept. 14, 1877.—Early this morning our genial friend, J. G. Heap, sent around a hack with Tom Jones as driver to convey our party to the mica mines.

"Tom is a clever, accommodating man with one leg shorter than the other, and when Dr. Hunt, Col. Killebrew and I got in, he cracked his whip over his

If he feels like taking the day off, he will probably pick up a chair, tilt it against the sunny side of the house, and start enjoying the day

mules and away we bumped. Up the creek, over granite and gneiss, quartz and stectite; why, this country is filled with geological specimens calculated to run a scientist crazy. Dr. Hunt, in spite of his obesity, was constantly jumping out of the wagon to examine something. He was in the greatest glee until he happened to find out our hack had a broken tongue, when his equanimity disappeared; thereafter his face was clothed in thunder.

"The farms bordering the stream were, as a rule, very good and each house was flanked by an orchard. The apples of the region are marvelous, and the bearing is prodigious. The peaches are just now getting ripe and are poor in quality. The rocks along this stream seemed to have melted and been poured out and stirred with a stick until it cooled. It twisted many a grunt from the two fat men of the party.

"At last we came to Mount Pezzle and alighting we began the ascent, holding on to bushes and pulling and toiling. It has ever been a matter of astonishment that mines should be built up in steep hills, or, being there, that fat men should visit them. The sun shone fiercely, no air stirred the leaves, and water was scarce.

"Lit up by the rays of the sun the waste of mica in the dump heap shone resplendently. All the hues of the rainbow were reflected, and it was difficult to divest the imagination of the fact that it was not gems that looked so enchanting.

"It occurs in this mine in a vein from six inches to three feet wide, and has its faces turned in every direction. Sometimes a piece will be taken out 18 by 24 inches. These slabs are taken to the shop and with wedges split open, until you get it thin enough to suit. It is blown out of the wall and hence such a pile of debris.

"These mines were discovered by Mr. Heap, the present owner, from the Indian diggings. Traces are distinctly visible where they have been in ancient times worked by some people, and stone implements are often found in them. One huge block has been removed from the mine, but was split up, and Mr. Heap worked it up, selling it for $2,000. He has some 15 or 20 separate mines and is constantly supplying stove manufacturers, lamp makers, etc. The refuse is sold occasionally to the makers of dynamite, and they have used it to blow up the rocks of the mines. It is ground into a coarse powder and then saturated with nitric and sulphuric acid, and dried. The powder can only be exploded by concussion and its power is enormous. Mr. Heap receives orders chiefly from stove makers and has it cut into the size ordered and ships it at from two to six dollars per pound. All the work done in these mines is cooperative. So much is paid for mining per pound, Heap furnishing the mines and the others the labor. It has been very remunerative and has been mainly instrumental in building up Bakersville. There is no visible limit to the split of these mica plates. You may split as long as you can see it, and then with a microscope you can keep on splitting until it disappears.

"We collected many valuable specimens and loaded down with them went down the mountain. Before we reached the hack a countryman overtook us, handing me a specimen. It was a valuable, large and beautiful garnet."

The concluding negotiations for the vehicle with the broken tongue are worth noting.

"'Tom,' says I, 'what do you get for your hack?'

"'One dollar a day.'

"'Why, that is the cheapest riding I ever did. One dollar a day! Well, well!'

"'Maybe, stranger, you don't understand hit. My hack gits a dollar, I git a dollar and my mules git a dollar.' And thus he adapted himself to my ideas of the price of locomotion."

Uncle Zack McHone of Chalk Mountain says he was the first Mitchell County man to send a piece of mica away and get money for it. He had heard that one could sell mica in Marion, and he finally discovered that mica was the same thing as the isinglass he had dug out of the ground, when he was a boy, to make playhouses for his little sisters. So he dug out a block of mica and ruined two handsaws trying to saw it into a neat square. It brought $7.75 in Marion somewhere about 1870.

In Spruce Pine, Isaac English, who hid the Union officers at the Yankee Rocks in war time, and Colonel Gere, one of the men whose life he had saved, went into partnership in the mica business. English was running an inn in a big log house he had bought from James Bailey that stood by the Toe River Ford at the crossroads of the Burnsville, Cranberry and Marion roads. He was squire now, and county surveyor, but mineralogy was his hobby. Part of his collection still lies between the logs on the porch wall of the old Hotel. During the reconstruction days he began to receive letters from an unknown correspondent who signed a single word, Gere. Nothing in the letters indicated why they were written. One day Alice Jane English, who had more curiosity than her husband, wondered if there could be any connection between the letter writer and the Yankee soldier who had given her a daguerreotype the night she gave him his supper in the cabin below Yellow Mountain. When she found the picture, it was signed with the same name as the one on the letters, Colonel J. M. Gere.

The identity of his northern correspondent established, English wrote to him at once, and before long Colonel Gere came South to visit him. He had written thus guardedly, without making direct mention of how he came to know English, for fear the letter might fall short of its destination and make trouble for English in the rancour of post war days.

As the two men walked up and down the hills together freely, in a country at peace, they came naturally to talk of English's hobby, the mineral wealth of the mountains. He showed his guest a sample of mica. He had no market for it, but he knew where there was plenty. J. G. Heap and E. B. Clapp were already making money selling it. Colonel Gere was interested at once. Connections were established for marketing, and the two men went into business. The Geres came to live at the Inn, and English added a new log upright which became the mica house of Gere and English.

With the opening of the first mines, men accustomed to living from the soil and trading hams, honey, sorghum, and corn, for salt, coffee, and snuff, came suddenly to know the feel of quick money. All up and down Toe River they burrowed furiously in the earth in untimbered, dangerous tunnels that were no more than overgrown ground-hog holes, until a cloud of dust seemed to hang over the mountains. Land holders wanted to know the exact location of boundary lines and discovered that ever since the huge colonial grants, men had been buying and selling with bland indifference to exactitude. There was endless litigation, sometimes bloodshed.

When Charles Dudley Warner passed through Bakersville and Burnsville in 1885 after his descent from Cloudland Hotel on the Roan, he saw the Toe River Valley when it was just beginning to realize its mineral wealth.

"The valley looked fairly thrifty and bright, and was a pleasing introduction to Bakersville, a pretty place in the hills of some six hundred inhabitants with two churches, three indifferent hotels and a courthouse. This mountain town, 2550 feet above the sea, is said to have a decent winter climate with little snow, favorable to fruit growing and by contrast with New England, encouraging to people with weak lungs.

"This is the center of the mica mining and of considerable excitement about minerals. All around the hills are spotted with 'diggings.' Most of the

The lost and forgotten gem-sorting house, a ruined pole cabin in the perpetual green twilight of the close thicket

mines which yield well show signs of having been worked before, a very long time ago, no doubt by the occupants before the Indians. The mica is of excellent quality and easily mined. It is got out in large irregular shaped blocks and transported to the factories, where it is carefully split by hand and the laminæ, of as large size as can be obtained, are trimmed with shears and tied up in packages for sale. The quantity of refuse, broken and rotten mica piled up about the factories is immense and all the roads round about glisten with its scales. Garnets are often found imbedded in the laminæ, flattened by the extreme pressure to which the mass was subjected. It is fascinating material, this mica, to handle, and we amused ourselves by experimenting on the thinness to which its scales could be reduced by splitting. It was at Bakersville that we saw specimens of mica that resembled the delicate tracery in the moss agate, and had the iridescent sheen of the rainbow colors, the most delicate greens, reds, blues, purples, and gold, changing from one to the other in the reflected light. In the texture were the tracings of fossil forms of ferns and the most exquisite and delicate vegetable beauty of the coal age. But the magnet shows this tracery to be iron. We were also shown emeralds and 'diamonds' picked up in this region, and there is a mild expectation in all the inhabitants of great mineral treasure. A singular product of the region is the flexible sandstone. It is a most uncanny stone. A slip of it a couple of feet long and an inch in diameter each way, bends in the hand like a half-frozen snake. This conduct of a substance that we have been taught to regard as inflexible, impairs one's confidence in the stability of nature and affects him as an earthquake does.

"This excitement over mica and other minerals has the usual effect of starting up business and creating bad blood. Fortunes have been made and lost in riotous living; scores of visionary men have been disappointed. Lawsuits about titles and claims have multiplied and quarrels ending in murder have been frequent in the last few years. The mica and the illicit whiskey have worked together to make this region one of lawlessness and violence. The travellers were told stories of the lack of common morality and decency in the region, but they made no note of them. And, perhaps fortunately, they were not there during Court week to witness the scenes of license that were described. This court week which draws hither the whole population is a sort of Saturnalia. Perhaps the worst of this is already a thing of the past; for the outrages of the year before had reached such a pass that by a common movement the sale of whiskey was stopped (not interdicted but stopped) and not a drop of liquor could be bought in Bakersville nor within three miles of it.*

"The jail at Bakersville is a very simple residence. The main building is brick, two stories high and about twelve feet square. The walls are so loosely laid up that it seems as though a colored prisoner might butt his head through. Attached to this is a room for the jailer. In the lower room is a wooden cage made of logs bolted together and filled with spikes, nine feet by ten feet square, and perhaps seven or eight feet high. Between this cage and the wall is a space of eighteen inches in width. It has a narrow door and an opening through which the food is passed to prisoners and a conduit leading out of it. Of course it soon becomes foul and in warm weather somewhat warm. A recent prisoner who wanted more ventilation than the State allowed him, found some means, by a loose plank I think, to batter a hole in the outer

---

*Of course Warner could not get liquor when no one knew him. In the same period Henry Franklin's grandfather, who entertained travellers at Linville Falls, used to keep a bucket of apple brandy sitting on the porch with a dipper in it.

wall opposite the window in the cage and this ragged opening, seeming to the jailer a good sanitary arrangement, remains. Two murderers occupied this apartment at the time of our visit. During the recent session of court ten men have been confined in this narrow space without room enough for them to lie down together. The cage in the room above, a little larger, had for tenant a person who was jailed for some misunderstanding about an account, and who was probably innocent, from the jailer's statement. This box is a wretched residence month after month while awaiting trial.

"We learned on inquiry that it is practically impossible to get a jury to convict a murderer in this region, and that these admitted felons would undoubtedly escape."

Warner could hardly help knowing about the land "quarrels ending in murder." The most sensational killing in the history of the district, the struggle for the Cebe Miller mine, which lies below the curve of the road at Flatrock between Spruce Pine and Bakersville, happened the year of his visit to Mitchell County. It ended with the death of three men and set an outraged army of citizens to combing every outbuilding, mine-hole, and rock cliff for the murderers.

The Cebe Miller mine was turning out as much as one or two tons of mica a day. It was located on land that was an entry of John Blalock's, but he never had surveyed it or completed the original claim, so after two years it had lapsed. Eventually the Penlands made entry for it, surveyed it, and carried out the requirements. No one was particularly interested in it until the mica excitement. Then Cebe Miller, who got his title from the Penlands, found himself with treasure and trouble. Ed Ray and W. A. Anderson, sons-in-law of Judge Bowman at Bakersville, cast envious eyes on the mine and were determined to have it.

They unearthed the old incomplete Blalock entry and, basing their claim on that, tried to dispossess Miller and those who worked with him. They planned first to get possession of the mine and then work it night and day while the Court decided on the rival claims. By that time, if they had to give it up, they would have practically exhausted the mica.

But Miller refused to be scared out. Instead, with Milt Buchanan, Steve Burleson, Bill Burleson, and Ed Horton, he went into the mine armed, and stayed there, working while they watched. Ray and Anderson made themselves comfortable outside on top, determined to starve Miller and his friends out. To add to the discomfort of the besieged men, the claim jumpers built smudges by the tunnel mouth and fanned the smoke inside, hoping either to drive the miners out or suffocate them. But the imprisoned owners failed to smother and managed to slip out from time to time at another opening to replenish their food supply. It looked as though Ray and Anderson were in for a long wait.

Then one Sunday afternoon Ray ran on to Cebe Miller near the shaft opening on one of his excursions into outside air. Ray pulled his gun. Miller ran at him with his fists and knocked him down the shaft with so terrific a blow that both of them landed on top of Milt Buchanan and the two Burlesons down at the bottom of the mine. They all grabbed Ray, four against one, and would have killed him outright, but he begged so piteously that they hesitated. He promised to go away and give up the claim—anything, if they would not kill him there in cold blood. Just then there was a shot above. They released Ray on his promise but kept his gun. He started up the ladder. As soon as he was a little out of their reach, he pulled another gun from his boot leg and fired straight into Miller's face. The bullet went just under the brain. His next shot killed Steve Burleson. Bill Burleson, his brother, got a ball through his shoulder. The shot aimed for Milt Buchanan missed. When Ray climbed out of the shaft he found Horton's body stretched on the ground with a bullet in his back, waylaid by Anderson as he returned to the mine with rations. Ray coolly threw the shells from his gun into the fire, reloaded, and disappeared. It was then about six o'clock in the evening.

The three dead men were carried into one of the old slave outbuildings that surrounded the M. P. Penland house, and everyone started after Ray and Anderson. The fugitives did not have much start, and it was a race between mountain men who knew the byways and pursuers who knew them too. The fury of the crowd almost cost the life of Judge Bowman, whose advice they believed to have been responsible for the Ray and Anderson claims. At last they ran the murderers out of Fork Mountain and turned them over, alive, to the authorities. The pair were tried in Caldwell County and jailed in Asheville—Anderson under conviction of murder, Ray, of manslaughter. On the night of July 3rd, Ray and Anderson, with two other murderers, forced J. R. Rich, the sheriff, and J. D. Henderson, the jailer, into a cell, bound and gagged them, broke the jail wall with an axe, and escaped. A military company was called out to hunt them, but they were never captured.

The truck that hauls spar on week days becomes a pleasure car on Sunday

If they could have known it, the mine that cost the lives of Miller, Burleson, and Horton and made two men fugitives the rest of their lives, was already practically exhausted when the struggle for the possession of it occurred. The rich mica vein worked by Miller at the start ended in a pocket that led nowhere.

General Clingman's coveted silver is yet to be found. The current tradition of a silver mine in the Unakas, or perhaps near the Roan at Magnetic City, keeps interest alive, and every now and then someone with a pick and spare time starts prospecting. Nobody can find it.

The most fantastic versions are abroad. Somebody's uncle knew half of the directions that would lead him to it, but the man who knew the necessary other half had gone to Tennessee or Texas or Kentucky. When he died, he told a friend how to reach it, but when the friend came to the mountains and located his inescapable partner, they quarreled, and neither would help the other. Each failed to find it alone. One version says that two men actually found it, with the help of a third man, but the man who had shown them the way would not go the last few hundred yards, and when they neared the opening, after leaving him, they heard such a fearful knocking in the middle of the earth that they decided to leave and go back another time. Of course they could never retrace their steps. In the late '80's counterfeit silver dollars, made of silver so pure that they were actually worth more than a dollar, were supposed to appear from Big Rock Creek near Magnetic City. Local people thought they knew who the counterfeiter was, and declared that he wore gloves because his hands were continually burned by the acids he used. At intervals he departed with his mule and came back with a load of silver. The rumor was never verified.

A stranger is pretty sure to hear about the silver mine if he stays long in Mitchell, in a version aptly suited to the teller's estimate of his credulity. Here is the story as I first encountered the tale.

THE SNAKE CHARMER

The Cherry Creek store shoulders up to the bridge
Right where they're building the road to the ridge
In a clutter of shale the blasting displaced
And thickets and sink holes with mud to the waist;
A camp for white labor; a small commissar;
And a prison stockade, beyond not so far;
And up in the laurel, a holler from here,
The cabin that houses the state engineer,
Strange to the mountains, and lately from town.
He wanted to learn things. Tonight he went down
Where the mountain men gathered at Cherry Creek store,
The ones who belonged there—a dozen or more.
The building was tiny and sagging and old
And bulging with customers, all it could hold.
He heard the hum of their voices inside
As he opened the door. Then the talking died.
He paused uncertain what to do.
There were nods here and there from the men that he knew
And then heavy silence. He wasn't prepared
To be so conspicuous. Everyone stared.
A man by the coal stove offered his seat.
He perched on it gladly and planned a retreat.
It was hard to face those appraising eyes.
The next box was empty, he saw with surprise.
The label was plain. That couldn't be right!
Who'd be so careless to leave dynamite

On the floor in a crowd, so close to the heat
Like coal or kindling under your feet.
He was startled from silence. "That's empty, of course?"
"Well, no," someone said. "Say, don't they enforce
Any rules about keeping explosives up here?"
"Sit still where y'are. 'Taint full, nowhere near.
The folks that mine spar call fur that stuff a sight.
We keep it on hand but we're keerful all right
That nobody sets on it. We leave it stay
Right handy like that and keep outer hit's way."
The state's engineer made his way toward the door.
At the counter he paused just a minute more
To look at the French harp lying there,
And trying it out he started the air
Of *Dixie-Land*, a random choice.
"Lay off that harp!" The high thin voice
Of an oldish man who stood by the wall.
"I'll tell ye, I kaint stand at all
To hear that kind of music play.
Hit hurts my finger. Now ye'll say
Hit's notion, but I'll swear hit ain't.
I kaint bear harp tunes. No, I kaint."
The hill men looked at the engineer.
He laid down the harp. "I say, that's queer!
If that's the case, why I won't play.
What makes your finger act that way?"
Somebody whispered, "Sit down a spell.
That's Audey McGuire. Get him to tell
How he hurt his finger if you can.
He's a mighty interestin' man."
And Audey said, "If ye want to know
How come my finger acts up so,
Hit started this way. I guess you've heard tell
How wild the hills was back a spell.
Bad Tom Gillis up Sugar Run
Was awful bad. The things he done
I kaint begin to tell ye now.

The trail stops by a log cabin in a clearing

Another time I'll tell ye how
He treated strangers that come along,
And his kin all swearing he ain't done wrong.
When he'd kill a man, he'd keep his hat.
Ten hats he had. I'll swear to that.
I didn't see them but one man did
And was right in the loft where he kept them hid.
That was a furrier come from outside,
And Gillis showed him, the time he tried
To collect some money that Gillis owed.
He got there too soon and Gillis knowed
In a day or two he could make enough
Counterfeit money to pay for the stuff.
Gillis was store keepin'. That was his line
Besides counterfeitin', and he had a mine
Of good silver ore, but we didn't know where—
(Bird Mountain, we thought, or somewhere near there).
Folks were waitin' fur Gillis to die

Before they started an earnest try
To find out where he was gettin' his ore,
And his corpse wasn't cold, I'll swear, sir, before
All the men in the country was climbing Big Bird
And searching each knoll and cove where they heard
That Gillis had ever been known to go,
And of course I was prospectin' too and so
I was climbing around that mounting one day,
And most of the daylight was frittered away
With combing the slopes from every angle
And nosing through brush and thicket and tangle
When I found a fault in the rocks that gave
Almost the look of the mouth of a cave.
A cave or a *mine*. I dropped on my knees.
I could worm inside by a real tight squeeze.
The opening widened as I crawled ahead,
Like a mine sure enough—and Gillis was dead!
Then I turned back a minute to look toward the light
And I almost died at the awful sight.
Snakes, sir! I'm tellin' ye. Snakes by the dozens.
Whole snake families, uncles and cousins,
Holding on by their tails like clothes on a line
In the entry way to the silver mine!
(If the mine was ever there at all.)
I ducked my head and eased to the wall
And a big gray snake with a stripèd back
Whose tail was up in a ceiling crack
Eased down and looked me spang in the eye.
I couldn't run and I didn't try.
I stared at him as he stared at me
And I swear I stared so poisonously
Pretty quick he couldn't stand no more.
He arched right back where he was before.
Then a big blue snake with a wrinkly hood
Had a look at me, and we stared mighty good.
I stared so mean, he backed off too,
And I kept on studyin' what to do.

There wa'nt an outlet I could find.
There were snakes before and snakes behind
And dangling snakes on either side
To block me any way I tried.
I'm tellin' you I thought right sharp
And then I remembered the old French harp
In my breeches like it always was.
I hauled it out first thing because
I'd always heard how a tune can quiet
And I started *Dixie* off to try it.
Hit was plain enough that wa'nt the thing.
Ye ought to seen them switch and swing
And hiss when they got in each other's way.
(Y'know that tune is pretty gay.)
And they'd tie in knots and jerk and spit.
They wrenched and pulled and curled and fit.
Where they'd been kind of still before
They was all a-squirm clar to the door.
Then something says, 'Try a slow hymn tune!'
And I changed my music, none too soon.
Almost Persuaded was what I played,
And one whole minute those big snakes stayed
As still as rocks. Then they started to swing
With a little soft hum like they tried to sing.
And they looked right nice as I crawled along
Blowing out hard on that grand old song.
I got pretty brave as I neared the door
And I stopped the music a minute before
I got clean out. Then I sure got bit
On my little finger. I shouldn't a quit.
And ever since, when I hear a harp
The pain goes rompin' mighty sharp."
Nobody spoke when the tale was done.
The the engineer said, "Did anyone
Ever find the mine? Was the silver found?"
"Not *yet*, hit ain't. Ye might look around."

The ceaseless drowsy splash of falling water

Cleared fields lose themselves in thickets

Mica has been the fairy godmother of Mitchell County. Men hunted for silver and gold and they found mica; they hunted for mica and they found gold and precious stones, feldspar, kyanite, uranium, and kaolin. The gold will probably stay in large deposits on Cane Creek until other, richer fields are exhausted; the gem mines are idle now, but they may be worked again any time as soon as foreign competition makes it worth while.

By 1894 a mine on Grassy Creek, originally operated for mica, gave up such fine gem-quality aquamarine that it was subsequently purchased by a company which worked it systematically. The Hungerford aquamarine mine lay just across the ridge, and the two developments furnished some of the finest stones thus far produced in the United States. The log sheds that stood above the mine are gone now, and the steep cleared hillside, shot with open-face craters rimmed with white, is overrun by a dense undergrowth that appears to have stood there forever. If you leave the Little Switzerland road at Wiseman's store, follow the lane that borders a valley field drowned with white clay overflow from a kaolin mine, and follow the trail through the woods by the right by-path, you can come straight to the black throat of the mine opening, walled in mica schist, with soda-spar crumbled almost to kaolin on the outer edges, a few of the big timbers still showing, and flawed golden beryl under foot. The main entrance is a dryad pool rimmed with slender leaning trees and dammed with glistening soda-spar, mica, quartz, and beryl crystals lost in the waste and weeds.

An emerald mine was discovered in 1894 by Bowman and Rorison near Boot McKinney's in the Crabtree district, seven or eight miles from Spruce Pine. While it has never yielded as well as the Wiseman and Hungerford operations, it is fully as romantic, and the dump yields more overlooked gem material because it is less accessible to visitors.

The quartz and feldspar which carry the emerald vein are penetrated in every direction by pencil-like hexagonal prisms, perfect in shape and of good color but sometimes too small for cutting with facets. A special ornamental gem material called emerald matrix has been developed by polishing these small emerald crystals *en cabochon* with the feldspar and quartz in which they occur.

Like the beryl operations, the emerald mines are abandoned today, but you can drive to within a hundred yards of the entrance tunnel if your car is not too low-hung to straddle the rocks that rear up in the road. The state highway is left behind, and the road lags lazily through the laurel, that edges back only enough for the wheel track to squeeze through to the high corn-fields and open roof of the sky. The hills crowd close in an intimacy of dreamy calm, and the mountains stretch to the sky line above. Then the trail sinks into shadowy thickets where the red clay never dries out and the ragged briers claw at the car windows. The road has a close secrecy and loneliness hardly dispelled by a solitary figure milking a cow in a fence corner or walking like a shadow along a lane. The trail stops by a log cabin in a clearing, where overalls are hung to dry on a line above a riot of wild aster and golden rod. Hay beans rattle in long strings along the porch wall, a serious fox hound stares from the path, and a few bunches of tobacco hang in the little pole shed.

A path leads past the door to an open wood of young trees fringing a narrow gully where three jagged mouths of the old mine open into the earth. The holes, which tilt downward in the direction of the path from the road, are full of water and give back no light. By the openings heaps of discarded ore, striated with black tourmaline, rotten garnets, mica schist, and flawed golden beryl give insecure footing. Apparently that is all of the emerald mines, and then one stumbles by accident upon the lost and forgotten gem-sorting house, a ruined pole cabin in the perpetual green twilight of the close thicket, sitting in austere privacy on a pile of rock stained with tourmaline and emerald crystals, with hand-made shakes and staring black window holes like the eyes of a skull, the floor in crazy angles dropped into the mud, the fireplace collapsed. The oldest part of the dump lies below the cabin. Once in a while, often enough to keep one looking with mounting excitement, there is the shine of green emerald crystals along the cleavage lines between mica schist and spar. They are worthless except as specimens in the matrix, or as a promise of better stones, perhaps overlooked in the discarded ore, perhaps sealed in the drowned dark of the shafts.

VIII

Buried Treasure

While the gem mines are losing themselves in the thickets, mica, feldspar, and kaolin keep pouring out of the Toe River country like the inexhaustible meal from the widow's barrel. They find their way into almost every home in the United States in one way or another, as scouring powder, china, pottery, glass, bathroom fixtures, and wall paper. They go into the manufacture of automobile tires, composition roofing, and electric flatirons.

As early as 1891 David T. Vance of Plum Tree began grinding mica in partnership with his brother, T. B. Vance, and H. R. Jones of Yumatilla, Florida. J. E. Burleson of Spruce Pine, who became the largest individual mica operator, began opening up mines about 1894, shipping mica by wagon load down the Blue Ridge. When the railroad provided a way out, he extended his holdings all up and down the river and built a mica house on top of Burleson Hill to take care of his output. The Poll Hill mines, Gibbs, Cane Creek, Birch, George's Fork, Henson's Creek, and River Mine at Penland were all Burleson operations. Eventually he owned mines from Ashe County, North Carolina, to Georgia. The Poll Hill and Gibbs mines in Mitchell County turned out over $500,000 worth of high grade sheet mica.

When the city of Cleveland put in the first electric lights, J. E. Burleson carried to Cleveland in a suitcase the mica to be used in the installation.

The Asheville Mica Company, founded in 1899, opened a warehouse in the Valley at Boonford on the new railroad in 1904, but it was four years before trains made the complete haul through the Blue Ridge to Marion. Until then much of the product had to be carried out in wagons. The Asheville Mica Company has a big stake in the Toe River country by virtue of the enormous holdings of its president, Vance Brown, who inherited two slices of the colonial Cathcart grant from his grandfather,—one for 99,000 acres, another for 50,000 acres, reaching the Three-Mile and Cranberry sections. Most of the surface has been sold, with the mineral rights retained. The Asheville Mica Company put up a warehouse in Spruce Pine in 1910, when the railroad had become a practical reality, and Gudger Fortner was put in charge. In 1920 they bought the J. E. Burleson mica business. The company has at times controlled as much as seventy-five per cent of the mica output of Mitchell, Avery, and Yancey counties.

J. E. Burleson and the Asheville Mica Company were mainly interested in buying and selling sheet mica in its original form. The decade from 1920 to 1930 saw the establishment of two mica processing plants in Spruce Pine, the Spruce Pine Mica Company and the Consolidated Mica Company, designed to cut special shapes for use in electrical installation from sheet mica. Up the river in Plum Tree the Tar Heel Mica Company operated by the Vances began turning out lamp shades from mica plate.

Side by side with the sheet mica business the ground mica trade was taking shape. There are two kinds of ground mica, muscovite (white) and biotite (black). The development of muscovite came first. The Vances in Avery County and J. E. Burleson in Mitchell ground scrap muscovite mica before 1900. Some time in 1906 Thomas A. English, Isaac English's son, who had an excellent power site to sell, interested Dr. Rouse, a visiting Pennsylvanian, in mica producing and grinding to such an extent that when he returned home, he made arrangements with Robert R. Dent, a broker, to promote a company. The English Mica Company, chartered in 1908, was the outcome of this visit. Dent eventually became so much interested that he took active charge.

At that time, whenever a motorist wanted to change a tire, he dusted the inside of the casing with non-adhesive powder before putting back the tube,

Now the mine is just a hole in the hill, with a cold breath blowing out of it

to keep it from sticking fast the next time he wanted to remove it. Probably it stuck anyway, but not quite so badly as if he neglected to powder it. Boys changing bicycle tires were worried by the same annoyance. One day when Robert Dent's son, Raymond, found his powder can empty, his eye lighted on a bag of ground mica, sent up from the North Carolina mill. The mica looked as if it would serve the purpose, so he used it. When he changed the tire again, a year later, the tube slipped easily from the casing without sticking at all. His father, who happened to be watching, asked what made the two rubbers come apart so easily. The boy remembered that he had used ground mica because the can of powder designed for the purpose had been empty.

The elder Dent reasoned that if ground mica was non-adhesive enough to resist sticking in a year's service on a boy's bicycle, it would work as well on an automobile tire. When he called on the Goodrich Rubber people in Akron and told them about it, they took a hundred pounds to try it out. In a few weeks they wanted five bags, then a ton, then a carload. Ever since then there has been a steady market for ground mica to be used to keep the inside form from sticking when the newly built-up rubber goes to the vulcanizing

The white scar of the Harris Clay pit is rimmed with its reddish overburden

oven. The accidental use of mica in a bicycle tire in 1911 now accounts for 40 per cent of the wet-ground mica industry.

In 1919 Robert Dent decided to buy and develop the biotite mine owned by Johnson and Gunter, which was producing a black schist that nobody knew much about. For five years the product was ground dry, designed for the roofing industry, but after the wet-grinding process was inaugurated in 1925, it has gone principally to the rubber trade.

Biotite mica is mined nowhere else in the world except in the belt running south from the Big Bald to Altapass in Mitchell County. Theo Johnson of Spruce Pine, who has spent his life locating mineral deposits, remembers that in 1908 his father, W. J. Johnson, showed him some of the soft flaky black mineral on the hill opposite and above Judge S. A. Martin's place. He ran across more of it sometime between 1909–1911 as he was surveying a line for Judge Martin in the Hanging Rock Valley. In partnership with his brother-in-law, Charles S. Gunter, he owned the land where he had first seen the black mineral, but neither of them knew what to do with it. About 1913 they persuaded Lethers Brothers of Howard, Pennsylvania, to look at the deposit, but nothing came of the visit. In the meantime, Gunter and Johnson wore out several sausage mills grinding the black schist themselves for experimentation, but they never sold any of it until 1918, when they got an order for three tons. At the time they were running a small muscovite schist grinding mill called the S. A. Martin Mica Company. Johnson sold out his share of the business to Dent in 1919, and started promoting the Victor Mica Company, which developed the muscovite schist on Tempe Mountain. The biotite order of 1918 was followed by another in 1919 for a carload. The biotite mill, built in 1920, is the only one in the world designed purely for grinding the black schist. Today the Spruce Pine district controls the entire output of biotite as well as fifty per cent of the domestic sheet and scrap mica business.

Until the railroad came into the Valley, there was no practical way to export heavy minerals. Gems and sheet mica, which are comparatively light, could be marketed, but not on any scale that required the moving of enormous bulk tonnage. Up until 1911 thousands of tons of feldspar went on to the dump. That year a sample carload of the hitherto worthless material was drawn by oxen from Flat Rock mine to Penland and shipped, each piece neatly dusted off with a whisk broom. In 1912, J. C. Pitman, working in the employ of W. E. Dibbel of Petersburg, Virginia, shipped the first commercial load of feldspar to go out of Penland, from Deer Park No. 1 mine on the James Bailey estate. The same year Theo Johnson and Charles Gunter sold to T. A. English and W. E. Blood the first carload to go out of Spruce Pine, which they had taken from the Water Hole Mine in Avery County. They cracked out all the mica, cleaned and sorted the ore, and got $2.60 a ton for it.

Spar, a cheap by-product of the well-established mica business, began to pour out of the district as fast as pottery, tile, glass, and soap manufacturers could take it. The producing period of a mine almost doubled, and so did the profits. As the market steadied, new mines were opened primarily for feldspar, with mica as a side line.

They belong to the mountain setting, these spar and mica mines with their straggling narrow-gauge dinky lines that ease through surprisingly narrow places to a hole in the hill with a cold breath blowing out of it and a pile of white ore dotted with waste sheet mica. If it is a large mine, there may be a tipple of logs. Often there is no more than the hole and the dump at the end of a wagon track.

If you skirt the white scar of the Harris Clay Company pit, rimmed with its

Feldspar grinding plants play an important part in Toe Valley life

reddish overburden, climb down the bank through the Tennessee Mineral yards, cross the river, and follow the dinky line that wobbles along the rocky river bank a mile or so, you will reach a log machinery house and a timbered hole in the bottom of a cup-like depression in the hillside that is the entrance to Deer Park No. 5. It is a well-timbered mine with a business-like stairway to the first levels. You light the carbide lamp on the front of your cap and descend into a cathedral-like cavern whose roof soars into the shadows, upheld by giant pillars between which the tiny points of electric bulbs wink like altar candles. After you have felt your way cautiously down the ladders that lead to the 300 foot level, you can pick garnets from the sheet mica just shot down with the spar. It seems as though everyone connected with the mines has his little box of uncut garnets, aquamarines, cairngorm, and moonstones.

In the early days of the feldspar industry, crude ore went to the grinding mills of the Clinchfield Products Company in Erwin, Tennessee, the first of its kind in the South. D. J. Grayson, a Pennsylvanian, was the original mill superintendent. The plant used batch mills for its fine grind and Hardinge mills for its 90 mesh coarse grind. The finest ore ground was the 140 mesh in comparison with today's 225 and 325 mesh. They had no air separator.

The McKinney mine has been turning out high grade spar for ten years

The Clinchfield Products Company presently had a rival in the Erwin Feldspar Company at Erwin, and another at Bristol in the Tennessee Mineral Products Company's grinding unit, all depending upon Toe Valley spar. Tennessee Mineral Products Corporation began operations in the district in 1921 by mining crude spar on the Wiseman properties on Beaver Creek. They abandoned the operation the following summer and in October obtained from Martin and Carter of the Blue Ridge Mining Company the lease of the Deer Park mines, originally worked by Dibbel. When they were certain that they had a dependable source of high-grade potash spar, they built a continuous grinding plant in Bristol, Tennessee.

The present commercial feldspar district in North Carolina extends throughout a belt of twelve to fifteen miles wide and twenty-five to thirty miles long, lying principally in the Toe River Valley. The feldspar from this area, produced in a multitude of small operations instead of by a few large mines, goes into the manufacture of floor and wall tile, pottery, china, glass, enamel, sanitary ware, soap, and scouring powder. Feldspar from the Spruce Pine district has held first place in the production of the country ever since the industry began. In 1931 the industry bulked fifty-two per cent of the total with an output of approximately 103,200 tons.

The North Carolina kaolin industry, developed by Colonel C. J. Harris of Dillsboro, began forty-five years ago in Jackson County, from where it gradually moved to the Toe River Valley as the rich deposits in the first field were exhausted. The Hog Rock mine, four miles southeast of Dillsboro, has been the richest mine in western North Carolina, worked primarily for kaolin. The deposit was so pure that it averaged sixty per cent recovery, as opposed to the sixteen to twenty per cent recovery in the Mitchell County field. The Hog Rock operation ran for twenty-eight years before it finally became exhausted.

Colonel Harris kept a shrewd eye on the whole belt lying west of the Blue Ridge, looking for new deposits as the Jackson and Haywood County fields became depleted. He knew there was plenty of kaolin in Mitchell, Avery, and Yancey counties, but he had little faith in it until the railroad opened up the country. Then he began to consider the Toe River district seriously as a possible field to take the place of the old one.

When Edgar Brothers of Metuchen, New Jersey, who had started a small clay operation at Penland sometime about 1906, wanted to sell their development in 1908, he bought them out. The Sparks plant at Minpro, farther up the River toward Spruce Pine, was started by Colonel Harris that same year and has been in continuous operation ever since. Today the pit has been worked 1200 feet in length with an average width of from 110 to 120 feet, and in some places to a depth of 130 feet.

In 1931 Carolina China Clay, which was organized by Harry Bailey, built a plant at the mine originally worked by Edgar Brothers, and began operations with seven clay deposits on the Bailey estate to draw on.

By 1925 the whole kaolin business had shifted to the Toe River district. The deposits are found mainly in small pockets, but they are numerous enough to total an enormous aggregate. While the output has never totalled more than 22,000 tons in its best year, kaolin brings a high price because it takes glaze well and holds a uniform color, and because its low shrinkage holds ware from warping when it is burned. Fred Smith, manager of the Harris Clay Company interests in the Spruce Pine district, estimates that there is enough clay in Mitchell, Avery, and Yancey counties to supply the needs of the pottery and tile business for a hundred and fifty years, basing his estimate on a production similar to that of 1928 and 1929.

IX

Spruce Pine

The coming of the railroad created Spruce Pine, which was to become the largest town in the Valley. The first railroad approached Mitchell County by fits and starts. Under the name of the old Three C it was built as far as Huntdale by 1900. By 1903 it had nosed its way the thirty miles to Spruce Pine, where it stopped again. George L. Carter was the promoter, backed by the Baltimore Trust Company.

Beyond Spruce Pine lay the wall of the Blue Ridge, which had to be tunneled if the road were to continue by the original plan to Spartanburg, South Carolina. The Baltimore Trust Company took a look at the confused steep ridges and figured the dismaying number of tunnels. Then they put the railroad up for sale. Carter bid the road in for the Thomas F. Ryan interests, but the Baltimore Trust Company refused to consider the sale legal, contending that Carter had no right to bid on it because he was a director of the company. Ryan employed Elihu Root to defend his purchase, and won his case in the autumn of 1904. By spring of 1905 he was ready for the tunnels.

When John Cox, later boss of Camp 3, came to Spruce Pine in the autumn of 1902 before the sale of the road, convict labor was being used to augment the force of native labor. At that time there were 160 convicts in the prison

The depot at Spruce Pine is the social gathering place where everybody turns out to see the trains

On Saturday afternoon the sidewalks of Spruce Pine are crowded

camp. The state withdrew them in January of 1903. After that, native labor carried on the work until the shut-down on July 4th necessitated by the controversy over the legality of Ryan's purchase.

The new management of the road was going to use free imported labor. All winter the country was on tiptoe expecting the new gangs. In northern cities company agents hired Italians, Germans, Russians and one Jew, and mobilized them in seven camps. There was work for the native Valley people, too, and a few Negroes found places for themselves. In all there were at least 2,200 men employed. A combination of either native and foreign or native and Negro labor is bound to prove explosive in the mountains, and things began to happen very soon. There were fights, and often murder. Usually the unaccounted-for "furriners" got the worst of it.

To Uncle Rube Mosley the past is only day before yesterday, but he seems to have been an old man for a long time. They were calling him Dad away back in the days when he carried mail to the labor camps that were building the Blue Ridge Tunnels.

"I was in one bad fight when I was with the railroad," he says, "and I had

They speak of themselves as the mountain people or the hill folks. "Mountaineer" is a hateful "furrin" word in Toe Valley ears

another special fight that was sort of private. I guess you know about the five Italians we shot at Camp 6. That's what we paid for. We found five dead, but there was more'n that. I don't know how many. Those five were buried under the chestnut by the Honeycutt tunnel, all lying in a row. We run 'em down, all that was footloose around the camp. Afterward I was standin' by the door of the commissary when it was all over and things got quiet, and a feller says to me, 'What do you figure those buzzards is after up yonside on the point?' And we went up to look and there was some more dead in a gully, lyin' all tore and mixed up. You know how they get.

"The morning hit happened I came up to Spruce Pine, turned in my mail, and loosed the mules in the corral. Hit was May 12th, 1906. Captain Cross came up to me and he says,

"'Can you use a gun?'

"'I can use one but I haint got one on me,' I says.

"Then he told me how he wanted me to help him put down a riot. I got Ed Brown's gun, rung me a handful of shells, and we went down the aisle of the 'Tally' shanties. (Camp 6 was in the loop after you come down off the Blue

Ridge and are startin' into North Cove.) Well, Captain Cross yells out to the men in the 'Tally' camp,

"'Go in your shanties and shut the doors.'

"That wouldn't leave nobody out but the insurrectors. When we got to Jimmy Mazone's (he was the ring leader), Captain Cross hollers for Jimmy to come out.

"'I'll give you five minutes to leave this camp,' says Cross, 'and four and a half of it's gone now.'

"Jimmy just looked at us. There was maybe eight with the Captain.

"'Me no go,' he tells him.

"I put up my gun then to shoot him and they begun firing from the house. They had lots of guns and ammunition, but they couldn't shoot to do any good. They was good with knives though. Well, after that you just had to do the best you could. Hit was us Americans agin the furriners. I didn't get a chance to kill Mazone because Neil Miller run him off. The first Italian to fall tipped right out of the door across my feet. The shooting was between six and seven in the evening.

"When hit was quieted down, Captain Cross said for me to see that nobody went in Mazone's shanty. But when John Cox came up that night from Camp 3, where he was boss, he tells me to help him bust the door down and see what was goin' on inside. I figured if he wanted to go in, we'd do it anyway, orders or not. So we smashed down the door. The 'Tallies' was inside all in a huddle, takin' on terrible. To hear them you'd believe they was all shot. Some was. One was shot through the neck and he died. One was shot in the heel, and two was dead. The rest of 'em just crawled around on the floor and kissed our hands.

"I turned in three guns I took to the company office, and W. D. Ledford turned in three. Later we both of us took a couple home because they belonged to dead Italians that wouldn't need 'em no more.

"I hadn't time to ask no questions when I got into the fight but when hit was American men agin 'Tallies,' of course I had to take up for the Americans.

"The way of hit starting was that this Mazone feller said he was hired by the company's agent to come down here as a foreman. If he couldn't be a foreman like they promised, he wa'n't going to work at all. The company says, 'We'll make you work.' He got things stirred up and I heard that some of the Italians had Cross's grave all marked off. They told him if he didn't get

The Black Brothers crowd next to Mount Mitchell in the Black Range

them money by six or seven o'clock, they'd 'make him sick at the neck.' So Cross had to have it out with them then and there.

"I knew something would come out of the shooting, and sure enough pretty soon I met a man with a warrant looking for me. I was just coming over the bridge in the ravine between the store and the boarding house. He started asking me questions right off.

"'Were you in the riot last night? Did you have a gun?'

"'You'll have to prove it,' I says. 'The Judge always told me I didn't have to say nothin' to incriminate myself.'

"My bond was all made out right then but I didn't know it. You see the company was fixin' to stick with me. Quick as I seen how things was going, I went to the cashier and asked for my pay so I could clar out.

"'I'm a family man,' I says, 'and I kaint pay nothin'. I'm an American man and I didn't intend to see the Italians kill the Americans, but now I'm done gone.'

"The cashier says, 'Stand your ground, Daddy. You ain't goin' nowhere,' and he wouldn't give me my pay.

"I told Captain Cross I was goin' to get clar of there, and he says, 'No, you ain't. Stand your ground and I'll take care of ye.'

"Captain Royce said the same thing, so I stayed. We had the trial at the commissary at Camp 6 the next day. Paul Johnston swore out the warrant on me (I didn't know it at the time) and then turned in with Will Pless and Hudgins to defend me. W. D. Ledford was tried along with me, and we were acquitted, only that wasn't the end of it. I had to go to Marion after a while for private examination, but they couldn't get anything out of me. I went kind of crazy and wouldn't answer nothing. [Uncle Rube shuts an eye slyly.] I haint tellin' nothin' when an American man's life is at stake to get him electrocuted.

"Finally they made me come to court down in Charlotte and I knew that down there I couldn't get away with nothing. Mazone was in jail and the Italian ambassador come down, takin' on, and hit looked like there might pretty near be a war.

"I was jammed in the back of the court room, scared stiff, and if I could a slipped out, I would. I kaint read but I knew what was goin' on when they called The State against Mark Baxter, W. W. McElroy and Carolina Company for Peonage, and he read out the law. When he said Carolina Company that meant me because I was workin' for them puttin' down the riot. When I heard Judge Biggs reading out that we submitted guilty, I felt my hair push up and I'd a give anything to just wormed out of there. The next thing he read judgment of $1000 and costs on Mark Baxter and $1000 and costs on W. W. McElroy and $1200 and costs on the Carolina Company. That was all there was to it. There was five Italians paid for (they compromised on $8000) and Mazone was turned loose."

Old memories, like noisy, bright birds half seen in a landscape grown dim, skim through Uncle Rube's head as he wears out the days safe and restless by the fire. When he thinks of the Blue Ridge tunnels that he helped to build, he sees long stubbly clearings in the brush, with niggers and strange white men pecking at the earth with shovels, the little board commissaries, mail bags, and a smashed hillside where dead men and mules are being carried out of a hole clogged with loose stone and dirt. Uncle Rube figures the cost of the Blue Ridge tunnels in lives.

Some of the road through the Blue Ridge, one stretch of which has nineteen tunnels in three miles, cost one million dollars a mile even with cheap labor. The first trains ran to Marion in 1908, but the way through the Blue Ridge had been open the year before. J. A. Mayberry, of Spruce Pine, remembers riding into Spartanburg on the first passenger train in 1910.

The railroad station on the north bank of the river drew stores and houses to itself like a magnet. Berry and Hickey, who had formerly been in a strategic point by the crossroads at English's, moved over the river to follow trade. The English Inn was like an old sailing ship washed up on the bank in a cove. It is a glamorous place of singing water and mossy bridges where the rhododendron bends over the cool brown stream like Narcissus in love with his own shadow, and the tangled grapevines wave gently in lost breezes that forever try to find their way out of thickets. Rank grass at the crossroads almost blots out the wheel tracks that curve into the undergrowth and vanish, the dirt is washed away from the roots of the spruce pine that stood on the bank at the intersection of the roads, and the ruined log sheds of the Inn yard, that used to be merry with jingling harness and stirrup and the staccato beat of hoofs, wait with caved-in roofs and doors ajar for the horses and wagons that never come.

In 1903 the only house on the other side of the river, where the railroad station, stores, and two hotels stand today, was the home of L. A. Berry. It stood in front of the present location of the Bank of Spruce Pine. Only a narrow stretch of ground between the lower slopes of Old Iowie and the

If the scheme of things is simple, it is no less satisfying

River is level enough for town building. The Berry house had to be moved to let the railroad by. The Holston Holding Company promptly bought 160 acres of the Berry land, covering most of the present site of the village, for $2,200. Sometime between 1903 and 1905 Uncle Taylor Phillips built a hotel with ten or twelve rooms on the north side of the river. The Turbyfills built another on the south side. Dr. Charles Peterson, who first came to town in 1907, put up the first brick building and the first drug store. When the Holston Holding Company was ready to sell its land after the completion of the railroad, John Cox, Dr. Charles Peterson, and Tom Byrd paid $17,000 for the 160 acres that were originally sold by Berry for $2,200. They had it plowed off into streets, and cut up into village lots. That same year the partners organized the Bank of Spruce Pine.

It was easy to name a town in those days. When the government in Washington was ready to establish a post office, whoever filled out the application blank wrote in whatever name occurred to him. Ledger, Day-book, Wing, Bandana, Lunday, Hawk, Plumtree, Staggerweed, Poplar, and a host of like names are scattered through Toe River country. Spruce Pine took its name from the tree that stood at the crossroads in front of the English Inn post-office.

By 1915 Spruce Pine was becoming a real village, linked to the outside world by the all-important daily train. The depot was the social gathering place where everybody turned out to see the train run. There was only one road where an automobile could be driven—the mile and a quarter stretch from the depot to the Burleson Mica House. J. E. Burleson had the first car to run on it, a Carter, friction drive. Dr. Peterson's Ford was the second. Twelve miles away, at the foot of the Roan Mountain, Bakersville was still the most considerable town in Mitchell County, as Burnsville was in Yancey. Down the river below Bailey's Peak, Penland was shipping more mica than any town in the United States. Altapass was promising to become the largest village in the three counties as a resort development fostered by the Clinch-field Railroad. At first the influx of population to the three counties had spread itself fairly evenly through the villages, but in the '20's the concentra-tion of the new mica, spar, and kaolin mills at Spruce Pine changed that. From 1918 to 1928 the population of the village more than quadrupled.

Until 1922 the two daily trains scarcely affected the character of life among the hill people. They considered themselves a separate entity. Anyone who comes from somewhere outside the mountains is a "furriner" in mountain parlance whether he comes from Knoxville or New York or London. They speak of themselves as the mountain people or the hill folks. "Mountaineer" is a hateful "furrin" word in Toe Valley ears.

The Toe River Valley had been a white man's country. The Blue Ridge, behind which lies the Toe Valley, looks like a fortress from the low country surrounding Marion in the Piedmont. The native people feel that it is just that, an outpost with customs of its own in a country with different folk-ways. They are willing to admit white furriners into their country-within-a-country, but they have no intention of being colonized by colored people. As long as the railroad furnished the principal way into and out of the Valley, the problem was negligible, but by 1922 improved highways were assured that would throw the country wide open. That meant the importation of Negro labor. The mountain people would almost rather not have the highway than let in the Negroes.

The contractors came in 1923 and brought colored labor gangs to work on the Spruce Pine-to-Avery County and Spruce Pine-to-Bakersville roads. The

Fiske Carter Company of Greenville, Tennessee, had charge of the Spruce Pine work, and Pat O'Brian's gang worked the Avery County section. The state established a convict camp and sent in more Negroes, and the Hawkins mine above the village of Spruce Pine took on colored laborers. The state road gangs and the convicts would go away when the highway was completed, but the Hawkins Negroes might be permanent if the temper of the district would stand it. Something was due to happen any day, and it did.

A Negro convict escaped from a prison camp and before he went far, attempted to assault a white woman. The driver of a truck who was hauling stone frightened him away before he did any harm, but he was not to be deterred from his purpose. Some miles away, about noon of the same day, he assaulted Mrs. Mack Thomas, Frankie Silvers' granddaughter, a woman sixty years old, who was going through the woods on the way to her son's home. As soon as her kinfolks found out about it, they started after him. The news spread so fast that everyone seemed to learn the details simultaneously. It was bad enough that the Negroes were on Toe River at all. This new outrage slammed down the switch on dynamite.

A mob came together before dark. It was like a storm rolling up in the far coves and flashing down the valley. The Negro who assaulted the white woman would have to be found, and then they would see that the rest of the niggers left the country. No more black men in Mitchell County.

L. H. Wright was chief of police for the town of Spruce Pine, A. N. Fuller, mayor, and Colonel D. W. Adams in charge of the Negro gang working on the streets. They had to bear the brunt of the uprising until help came. Mrs. Thomas was assaulted September 26th. That night Chief Wright was in the Altapass section on the trail of the convict Negro, expecting him to hop a freight near the Carolina, Clinchfield and Ohio yards. As he was midway in the Blue Ridge tunnel, the police chief met the coal drag and nearly suffocated with the fumes. That was only the start of the night. By twelve o'clock, when he got back to Spruce Pine, he found out from Herbert Hickey, a townsman, that a mob had gone to the Hawkins mine to round up the Negroes. They were on their way back, and would certainly go for the thirty blacks in Colonel Adams' street gang that was camped on the south side of the river. The mob was drinking and getting more violent every hour, and some of the street Negroes were likely to be killed.

The present cement bridge over the Toe River had not yet been built. There was a narrower one that crossed up above, nearer the town. The

From the Tennessee side one enters the Valley by a winding road between the Yellow Bald and the main crest of the Blue Ridge

confused shouting of the mob could be heard approaching the bridge along the track. The mayor, Colonel Adams, Hickey, and Wright held a hurried conference. It must be stopped if possible. When the crowd surged up to the bridge, Fuller, Hickey, and Adams mingled with the men, trying to reason with them. Chief Wright stayed on the bridge to hold them back if they rushed it. His twelve-year-old son was with him, but there was no opportunity to get him to a place of safety. When the mob tried to pass Wright the first time, he met them reasonably without showing a gun, and begged them to let the innocent Negroes alone. He gave his promise that in the morning every one should be sent away. The mob fell back, commenced to straggle, and then unexpectedly rallied. They rushed the bridge again, fell back, and came a third time with cries of "Shoot him down." Someone in the crowd fired both barrels of a shotgun at Wright, but the man beside him struck up his arm and the shots went wild. The chief held the bridge and continued to hold it.

Eventually the mob agreed to go away if two of their members could cross the river and tell the Negroes to leave. The black street gang left the next day by train, badly frightened but unharmed. The mob was not yet through clearing out the Negroes. They rounded up Pat O'Brian's gang of forty, knocked them around considerably, and shipped them out of the country in box cars along with the twenty from the Hawkins mine and the thirty in Colonel Adams' camp.

Troops arrived on September 28th, 1923, just one hundred and forty-three years after the Revolutionary soldiers had passed through Spruce Pine on their way to the battle of King's Mountain. They fortified the promontory across the river facing town, trained machine guns covering the business section, dug trenches, and patrolled the streets.

The *Asheville Citizen* for the morning of October 4th carried the following comment:

TROOPS MAY STAY IN MITCHELL
UNTIL TRIAL OF NEGRO IS OVER
Good Citizens Resent Disorder

Spruce Pine, Oct. 3.—Out of the trouble of the past ten days resulting in guardsmen patrolling the streets for the first time in the history of Mitchell county, is emerging a spirit that promises to be a great factor in the economic conditions in Western North Carolina—namely, that capital mining the natural resources is entitled to use negro or foreign labor to develop these resources.

The majority of residents of Spruce Pine have been bitterly opposed to the forced exodus of negroes. They have outwardly condemned the acts of violence and have given every consideration and courtesy to the troops on duty.

With the identification of John Goss, escaped negro convict trusty by Mrs. Mack Thomas who was assaulted Wednesday, Sept. 26th, as her assailant, plans are being made for a speedy trial. The scales of Justice will balance. If the negro is adjudged guilty by twelve fair-minded men, he doubtless will face the electric chair and death, and residents of Mitchell County appear satisfied with the knowledge that justice will prevail.

Since the arrival of troops Spruce Pine has been outwardly quiet although an undercurrent of reports have been closely investigated and all preparation made to prevent any further disorder.

Four negroes returned to work today bringing the total to about thirty and the community and surrounding territory is apparently satisfied for them to work. The capture of John Goss and the arrival of troops have had an important effect.

Visitors thronged the towns today to attend the Toe River Fair. The glitter of tinsel on Carnival dolls is seen on every hand. Many of the number carrying guns during the brief period of disorder are now repentant.

Word that warrants were being issued for the leaders of the mob has been received with alarm in the rural districts where the majority of the mob members reside.

Civil authorities are confident that the attitude of repentance of their acts, on the part of the leaders of the mob forcing the negroes to leave, is sincere and have faith in the future peace of the community. Rumors of possible violence and attempts to molest the negroes returning to work are beginning to quiet down. The presence of troops is the only sign of past disorder in Mitchell County. . . . General Metts, Major E. P. Robinson, in active command of the troops, as well as other officers and enlisted men have made friends of the residents of Spruce Pine. Those inclined to take the Law into their own hands have a new reverence for the National Guard.

The Negro who precipitated all the trouble was carried to Raleigh for safe-keeping until his trial in Bakersville at the spring term. A heavy guard attended his return and assured a peaceable trial. Judge Finley presided, with Johnson J. Hayes as solicitor. The defendant was found guilty, and electro-cuted at Raleigh. That court was memorable for more than the Negro trial. At least a hundred participants of the mob were tried for rioting, but were released with costs and small fines upon Chief Wright's petition for leniency. The mob had this in its favor. None of the Negroes had been killed, although they might easily have been wiped out. Through all the confusion of mob passion the people of Toe River had kept sight of their original purpose, to run the blacks out of the country. The state had carried its point and demon-strated that Negroes have a right in the mountains, but the hill people showed so unmistakably what their reception would be that since then the Negroes have not wanted to come up Toe River.

CHAPTER

X

" 'Light and Hitch"

Invariably a newcomer passes through three stages before he can say, "This is my country." After the initial rush of enthusiasm for the spectacular beauty of the mountain subsides and the picturesque is becoming natural, he chafes at the differences. He wishes there were more houses for outsiders, and more cellars, and warmer floors, and plumbing planned for cold snaps; and that it was not fifty-six miles to the stores in Asheville, and sixty-five to those in Johnson City, and that there were more than two trains a day. He hears tales of a cutting at a chicken fight, with someone hustled off to a hospital, of a couple of deputies exchanging shots with a flying figure near a rifled freight car, or of a spirited encounter at a still, and he remembers the uneventful order of some other place. He forgets that he himself is being permitted a perfectly orderly existence here, and that elsewhere there are occasional irregularities. He does not know how to react to the mountain music, because it is different, and he feels that the difference is wrong because his standard is still that of his own folk-ways.

Then, because he cannot possibly go on saying "No" to all the alien customs, the outsider gradually becomes indifferent to his surroundings, passing into a stage of passive disapproval. He stops making conscious evaluations and lives a day at a time.

Finally, if he stays long enough, some day something happens that pushes him over the edge into an acceptance of hill living. Maybe it is a trip to the place where he came from; perhaps he is annoyed because he hears a guest criticize a condition he had once remarked about himself; maybe it is just being alone sometime and looking at the hills and finding that he does not struggle any more against the changes they have made. Then he can say, "This is my country."

Cecil Sharp, the English ballad authority, visited the neighborhood of the Toe River country with Olive Dame Campbell while they were preparing the material for their book on mountain ballads. Although he overestimates the length of the isolation period, he gives an excellent general picture of how the mountain people looked to an Englishman in 1915, when the outside influences were still outside.*

"The region is from its inaccessibility a very secluded one. There are but few roads—most of them little better than mountain tracks—and practically no railroads. Indeed, so remote and shut off from outside influence were, until quite recently, these sequestered mountain valleys that the inhabitants have for a hundred years or more been completely isolated and cut off from all traffic with the rest of the world. Their speech is English, not American, and, from the number of expressions they use which have long been obsolete elsewhere, and the old-fashioned way in which they pronounce many of their words, it is clear that they are talking the language of a past day, though exactly of what period I am not competent to decide. One peculiarity is perhaps worth the noting, namely the pronunciation of the impersonal pronoun with an aspirate—'hit'—a practice that seems to be universal.

"Economically they are independent. As there are practically no available markets, little or no surplus produce is grown, each family extracting from its holding just what is needed to support life, and no more. They have very little money, barter in kind being the customary form of exchange. . . .

"They are a leisurely, cheery people in their quiet way, in whom the social instinct is very highly developed. They dispense hospitality with an open-

*Introduction to *English Folk Songs from the Southern Appalachians*, collected by Olive Dame Campbell and Cecil J. Sharp. Courtesy of G. P. Putnam's Sons.

handed generosity and are extremely interested in and friendly toward strangers, communicative and unsuspicious. . . .

"They have an easy unaffected bearing and the unself-conscious manners of the well-bred. I have received salutations upon introduction or on bidding farewell, dignified and restrained, such as a courtier might make to his sovereign. . . . The mountaineer is freer in his manner, more alert, and less inarticulate than his British prototype, and bears no trace of the obsequiousness of manner which, since the Enclosure Acts robbed him of his economic independence and made of him a hired labourer, has unhappily characterized the English villager. . . .

"Physically, they are strong and of good stature, though usually spare in figure. Their features are clean-cut and often handsome; while their complexions testify to wholesome, out-of-door habits. They carry themselves superbly, and it was a never-failing delight to note their swinging, easy gait and the sureness with which they would negotiate the foot-logs over the creeks, the crossing of which caused us many anxious moments."

The most salient trait an outsider notices when he comes in contact with the mountain man is his all-embracing hospitality. He greets you with "'Light and hitch!" or "Come in and warm," or "Set down and cool off," and urges you to stay for dinner. When he leaves your house, more than likely he says "Come home with me!" as the formal phrase of parting. And he means it. Unless the home is a very poor one, the storage cellar back of the house holds enough country hams, Irish potatoes, yams, jars of pickled beans and sauerkraut and canned fruits to take care of half the congregation at the churchhouse, should they drop in unexpectedly.

The outsider finds himself continually reversing his first impressions. The mountain man whom he sets down as naïvely unsophisticated because he asks all sorts of artless questions turns out to be unexpectedly complex. The newcomer discovers by intuition, if he is surprised into confiding more than he intends, that it is the mountain man who thinks *him* simple. The obsolete words and phrases of the back country have an honorable origin in Elizabethan English, and the mountain speech is the result of tradition, not ignorance.

As the outlander lives among the hill people and knows them better, he marvels at their splendid poise and lack of self-consciousness. The explanation may lie in their blood, that is Scotch, Irish, and English, with here and

His old-fashioned speech has an honorable origin

The building where Roby works was never intended for anything more than a shelter for the corn mill and a support for the water-wheel

there a dash of Pennsylvania Dutch, but it may be the cultural legacy of long years with time to think, coupled with general acceptance of their environment and the refusal to take economic pressure seriously. There is something to be said for small houses, and farming that requires only part of the day. These people do not make elaborate preparations to enjoy life but begin at once, and if their scheme of things is simple, it is no less satisfying. A mountain man will hardly slave through a sunny spring day when he longs to enjoy the weather in order that he may take a vacation in the same sunshine somewhere else later on. His affairs are not so pressing. As soon as he thinks of it, he will probably pick up a chair, tilt it back against the sunny side of the house, tip his hat down over his eyes, and start in on the business of enjoying the day.

Instead of suffering stage fright, hill people enjoy an audience. Some time ago the women who weave in their homes for the Fireside Industries of the Appalachian School gave a short play at a summer pageant on the green before the long double porch of Ridgeway Hall. The stage properties were necessarily simple. There was no actual stage at all, and yet those women,

Roby Buchanan works in a one-room mill tucked away among alder bushes

mothers of families and unused to seeing plays, much less act in them, gave a surprisingly good performance. They were so completely natural that the illusion which the play proposed to create was convincing.

Doc Hoppas of Brushy Creek, much in demand locally as a story teller and ballad singer, will sit down in a chair in front of two or three hundred people at the Appalachian School festivals and tell stories and sing as nonchalantly as though he were on his own shady porch. In the summer of 1933 he told mountain tales and sang ballads from the door step of the Carolina Cabin which the Penland Weavers sent to the Century of Progress Exposition, and he enjoyed giving the performances quite as much as his audiences enjoyed hearing them.

One day when we were living in a cabin on Conley Ridge back of Penland, I took my little son to a neighbor, Mrs. Coley Dixon, to leave him while I went to Spruce Pine, seven miles away, to attend a club meeting. Mrs. Dixon was a tall mountain woman, crippled with rheumatism, but a fine cook and housekeeper, who pieced quilts that might be museum pieces. She was heating two little flatirons on the hearthstones and ironing a long piece of blue denim on a board laid over the bed in the living room. When I asked if she would look out for the boy, I happened to mention that I was going to preside at the meeting and dreaded it.

Mrs. Dixon stopped ironing in honest surprise, saying, "Well, that beats me! Looks like when you got such a perty new dress on you could just rare back and face 'em down."

The mountain man seems able to adapt himself to any kind of job, even create his own tools if necessary. He may not work at it long, however, if something else claims his interest. My neighbor on the Ridge could move or repair our telephone, lay stone, do mechanical work on the car, cut and split wood, chink logs, underpin a house, or do any ordinary kind of farm work.

When, as a boy, Doc Hoppas wanted a banjo, he made it out of a wooden axle-grease box, using waxed shoe threads for strings. Besides being a ballad singer and story teller, he is a spar miner, stump puller, farmer, woodsman, barber, and maker of axe handles. When he saw his wife laboriously thread-ing bobbins for her loom, he made a machine to do it for her, and he devised a hooped trellis of hickory bark laced between saplings for the bean vines to climb, so she could stand in the shade to pick them.

Roby Buchanan, who lives in a cabin at the head of the narrow Cane Creek Valley, where Lightwood Mountain and the Mine Fork Rough crowd up to

The hill man takes education seriously, because he has to work for it
if he gets it

Hawk Mountain, taught himself to cut and polish gems and made almost all his own equipment. He has taken particular delight all his life in choice minerals, and whenever he could spare money, he sent away bits of gem quality garnet, beryl, and amethyst to stone cutters for polishing. He wanted a large representative collection of the gems of the mountains, but while he could get the rough mineral, the cutting was so expensive he could not afford very often to have a stone polished.

So, living on his secluded farm with no one to help him, he learned to do it himself. He managed to wade through all the government bulletins he could find on that and related subjects, learning the elements of the trade painfully by trial and error with his home-made equipment, writing to other gem cutters to ask questions he could not solve, and slowly improving his work-manship. No one man would tell him all he wanted to know, but he kept learning until now he is on the way to realizing his collection of native gems and has branched into other minerals not native to the district.

Roby Buchanan works in a one-room mill tucked away among alder bushes, with a water-wheel as tall as the building, in the field just behind Hawk Post Office. The gem-cutting equipment is at the right of the entrance, by a small sunny window, with the mill on a raised platform in front of the door, and under the roof the wooden lever that switches the sluice water on to the wheel or away from it. The water power serves the gem wheel as well as the corn mill. The air is full of the sweet grainy corn dust, and over it hangs the ceaseless drowsy splash of falling water as the shadow of the big wheel passes and repasses the window up under the roof.

Aquamarines, garnets, landscape agates from Hawk Mountain reminiscent of Japanese brush paintings, smoky topaz, moonstones, sunstones, rutilated quartz—like water pierced with straws of gold—rose quartz, cairngorm, and amethysts, he has found for himself; opals, chrysoprase, turquoise, tiger's eye, jasper, and malachite he has bought and polished. He carries them all around in an old cigar box, each wrapped in a bit of copy paper fastened with paper clips. There will be a remarkable collection of gems in that cabin as time goes on. Roby is a comparatively young man now, lean-faced and eager at thirty-five, married, with a couple of sons growing up.

One has a special feeling for a stone that he has seen first in the rough and whose polishing he has watched. When I finger my little cabochon of thulite I see a shiny white stone with irregular pink markings, the color of the inside of a sea shell, but I see, too, the rain pouring down on Cane Creek on a windy autumn morning and Roby splashing down the road on the heavy farm horse in a great hurry, his black rain coat glittering like patent leather. He wants to cut off the sluice from the water wheel lest it go too fast after the night's downpour. Wet gusts puff in at the broken windows of the mill and wet the clean new meal in the open box below the hopper; the fire sings up the rusty chimney that sits carelessly over the stove hole, leans backward unsteadily toward the wall, and disappears through it abruptly without ascending to the roof.

As Roby works over the piece of thulite we have brought, roughing it out to shape, polishing it on a poplar disk, on leather, and felt, the room roars with the great splashing of the water wheel, spinning with full pockets, and the fusillade of rain on the roof. He runs up the steps to the mill platform, pulls the lever that regulates the water, and the big wheel out of doors spins to a stop. As soon as the gem wheel is changed for the next operation, he jumps to the platform and turns on the water wheel again; the little disc

Mountain men and women in isolated valleys who realize the handicap of their own schooling have given their children the best they can afford

whirs and the thulite shines through its smear of carborundum. In less than an hour it lies in my hand, oval, newly washed, and shining.

It was inevitable that Roby would want to learn to cut faceted stones as soon as he had mastered the art of polishing *en cabochon*. Again, because of lack of funds, he must take the longest way around. He could not buy a faceting machine outright. He might make one as he had made his polishing outfit. After six months of study he had his design. Then he went to Greenville, South Carolina, and had a machine constructed from his drawing. It worked as he hoped it would, and he brought it back with him in triumph to Cane Creek to set up in his corn mill.

New difficulties immediately presented themselves. When the water power is attached, the turning of the big wheel shakes the building and with it the gem-cutting machine. It is difficult enough to judge the depth to which the facets should be cut without the added complication of standing on chattering boards before a jiggling machine. Added to that, he must cut by daylight inasmuch as his plant boasts no lighting facilities, and in the daytime, as long as he is running a custom grinding mill, he must grind corn for all comers. Frequent interruptions do not affect cabochon polishing more than to delay the completion of the process, but they do complicate the work with faceted stones, depending upon mathematical changes of angle. Nevertheless, the corn-grinding business must be nursed along to make the gem-grinding business possible, and so after ten or fifteen minutes at the gem machine, Roby philosophically slips the belt off the wheel and turns the water power to the corn mill, measures out his own share for the grinding from the corn the customer has brought, and dumps the bag of grain into the hopper.

The building where he works was never intended for anything more than a shelter for the corn mill and a support for the water wheel, but it is the only place he has for his gem equipment. It will have to serve. If the faceting machine dances about when the power is applied, he will learn to make allowance for it. And somehow he manages to turn out cut stones that average very well with those done on more pretentious equipment.

The hill man takes education seriously because he has had to work for it if he got it. Those of the people who are illiterate are not so because they wanted to be. Some of them grew up at a time when the school system had utterly broken down, and the best their parents could do for them was to pass on by word of mouth what they themselves remembered. Now when there is money in the country, these men and women who missed their chance have provided as good equipment as they can afford for their children. The 1929–30 educational report for Mitchell County lists buildings and equipment worth $263,975 with 3,395 white children and 8 Negroes going to school. Yancey County has a total enrollment of 4,147 and buildings and equipment worth $154,275.

The mountain man can stand a hard job in cold or wind or rain as long as the end is in sight when he can start something else, but he chafes at a monotonous, comfortable job that involves no individual struggle and holds over from day to day and week to week. Hardiness that scorns weather, hunger, and fatigue is part of the mountain ideal, not plodding busy-ness just to be doing something. The winter night when our radio first came to Conley Ridge was an occasion for native pertinacity.

To get to our cabin a car had to follow the state highway toward Bakersville over Flatrock hill and then turn into the Penland road, narrow and winding but with a rock foundation. The Ridge road had not yet been improved except for a coating of spar on the steep spirals that loop back and forth to

Hardiness that scorns weather, hunger, and fatigue is part of the mountain ideal, not plodding busy-ness just to be doing something

A cloudless day on Spring Creek, marked by the easy rhythm of grinding cane

make a cramped ascent to Ridgeway Hall. On the mountain top real trouble began. The road, which was of red clay and apparently without bottom, circled a high valley, keeping to the ridge line, where there was a prospect of sliding down into the fields if the car jumped out of the ruts.

We had been promised that our radio would be sent up sometime during the day on Saturday, but when it had not arrived by supper time, we gave it up and went to town for supplies. There was a light rain falling and the road was thawing and muddy. We spent a couple of hours in town, and then, before we left for home, we went to the music store that was sending the radio to see why it had not arrived. The owner told us that his men had been up during our absence and found the cabin locked, so they had come back down. They had had quite a bit of trouble negotiating the muddy loop on the Ridge. However, he offered to send the radio back again that night so we might have it for Sunday, his light truck to follow our car.

It was about nine o'clock by that time, and the rain pelted in front of a stiff wind. The lights of the truck followed us closely to the climb up the Ridge, which our car took faster than the other. We started the long, muddy pull

Steam from the boiling sorghum rises into the crisp October air

Cane boiling is a family affair

The wife keeps the little house clean without spending much time at it

around the loop alone, going slowly and watching for it. We were on the last lap when we saw the lights of the truck wavering in the worst stretch of road across the valley from us. As soon as we reached the cabin we built a big fire in the fireplace so the men would be able to dry out when they came. Then we sat down to wait, watching the road line on the ridge across the valley. No lights appeared, and finally at midnight we decided that they must have found the road impassable for the truck and started back to Spruce Pine.

The next morning we were awakened about eight-thirty by someone hammering on the door. It was bitter cold; the rain had stopped and everything had frozen hard. There on the kitchen porch were the radio men, their faces purple with cold and the car plastered with mud. They had spent the night in the wind and rain without shelter, and yet they arrived perfectly agreeable and smiling.

On the night before, when they entered the first stretch of clay road where the mud flowed like a creek, they had slid down into the field and were unable to get back out again. The lights of their car were hidden in the bushes which prevented our realizing their trouble, and although they knew that the main building of the Appalachian School was not far behind, they felt they could not leave the radio and tools. So they built a little fire and sat by it all night. As soon as light came, they repaired the car but were unable to get it back into the road. Undaunted they came across the valley, making their own road, and thus arrived at our house some eleven hours after they had started from Spruce Pine. They had had no supper the night before, what with their two trips to the Ridge, but they protested they were not hungry when I hurried to cook their breakfast.

Any estimate of native character must take into account an elemental rashness and precipitancy which, coupled with oversensitiveness and a short temper, may develop unexpected complications at any time. Two northern girls who were my guests had gone on an all-day trip to the top of Roan Mountain in company with two boys from Toe River. They came back in a high state of fury, minus one of their escorts. It turned out that on the trip up the mountain one of the boys had stopped for corn liquor and after that had driven like mad over the steep road which humped into boulders every now and then. Upon their arrival at the top he had drunk a whole pint by himself before starting down from Carver's Gap. They had made a record descent from the mountain, expecting to be dashed to pieces every minute. Some of the tires blew out, hub caps were knocked off, a dog was run over as well as a couple of geese, and corners were skirted on two wheels before they reached the bottom safely. There they hailed another car and left their driver. Next morning both girls were black and blue from swinging against the sides of the car as it catapulted down the mountain.

The first time I saw the boy I asked him, "What made you drive like that? You might have killed them."

He smiled his disarming smile and said, "I know it. Right then I wouldn't have cared if I had either. They just hawked hell out of me with their everlasting talk."

That boy was one of the fastest, most reckless drivers I have ever seen over roads that turn on themselves in incredible curves, and yet I never knew him to have an accident. Even after stiff drinking he brought the car down one of the most hazardous roads in the country at an unbelievable speed and never made the marginal calculation wrong. The young men of the hill country, while often spectacular and fast drivers, are also apt to be very good drivers. When I first came into Spruce Pine it was by way of Elizabethton and Cranberry over the curving Avery County road. In my naïveté I thought, as we circled up unfenced shoulders above steep slopes, "It can't be that people drive much here after dark." Later I rode over those same curves in a roadster at sixty miles an hour, feeling the car start to tip and right itself each time.

Mountain loyalty is romantically intense and has an important bearing on the relations of employer and employee. In the first place, the mountain man does not consider that he goes to work for another man as his servant. He comes to help him out, and he will continue helping as long as he likes his employer and finds the job interesting, provided that economic pressure at home demands his working for someone. While he remains on the job, he will be fiercely partisan in his employer's interest. A few years ago, when the manager of a mica grinding plant became involved in a lawsuit where feeling was running high, three of his men came to him severally of their own accord saying, "Would hit holp you if that other fellow wa'nt able to come to court?"

The mountain man's conception of loyalty transcends considerations of right and wrong. He thinks he ought to stick with you especially if you are in the wrong because then you will need help the most, but he expects you to do the same by him.

Outsiders are apt to complain bitterly of the impermanence of their native white domestic help. It is not hard to explain, in view of the native character, considering that the economic pressure on a mountain girl is not very heavy.

When she comes to help in a house in town, she does not expect to stay past the time when she gets her clothes fixed up or when she has helped tide the folks at home over some emergency that calls for money. At first, water that runs hot and cold from a faucet, the electric equipment, and the bathrooms are delightful novelties that make up for missing the free, easy-going life at home and the companionship of her brothers and sisters; but then she discovers that she hates to do the washing indoors even with all the convenience of the glittering water faucets, remembering the pleasant mornings boiling the wash kettle by the branch side. She has less time to herself now, even with all the handy things to use in cleaning, because there is so much more house to care for and such a fearful lot of useless dusting. Her mistress tries to make her use a dust pan instead of sweeping the dust from room to room and then down the porch steps or into the cellar-way, and she will not let her entertain her boy friends in the day time. Supper is too late. When her mistress thoughtlessly gives a direct order, she makes it clear with a level look that she is only "helping." No great demand is made upon the fundamental loyalty that would keep her working, because by this time she probably does not like her mistress very well, and then one of the least 'uns at home "gets took down," or her mother wants her for hog-killing or berry picking or hoeing, and she is gone.

In their conception of what is necessary there is a fundamental difference in the minds of outlander and native which makes it hard for them to understand each other. Both make a fetish of time, but in order to use it in a different way. The outlander wants to employ his time—to sell it for money so he can buy the things he believes he must have. A job is of paramount importance. The native wants time as leisure, and he can get that without money by reducing his scale of wants to a minimum. He knows pretty well how far he can go along that line. The outlander spends time converted into money; the mountain man spends time itself.

CHAPTER

XI

"I Got a Girl on

Sourwood Mountain"

When a mountain boy slips up beside the girl he likes after "preachin' has broke" and escorts her up the road home, her friends say she is "talkin' to him." That is the first stage in courtin'. When he comes and takes her to the church-house and calls on her with presents of candy and Victrola records, they have advanced to the sparkin' stage.

Lovemaking is an occupation that can engage a mountain man's undivided interest. He is a demanding and passionate lover, but the rugged mountain girl is a match for him. Perhaps he overpersuades her and they "plant their corn before they build their fence"; if he fails to marry her, the child she bears out of wedlock will be a "woods-colt." The girl's family may force the boy to marry her through the courts, but if he runs away, or if, as sometimes happens, she decides she does not want to marry him, she remains at home and brings up the baby along with her young brothers and sisters. The general attitude is that while a sin has been committed, there is no use taking it out on the child. The irregularity is remembered, but it is seldom dis-

The hill man has an easy bearing

cussed, although sometimes a newcomer is surprised by seventeenth-century frankness if the subject comes up accidentally.

A friend of mine was entertaining a five-year-old child one morning who informed her brightly that a new baby had arrived down the road the night before.

"What is it?" asked the woman, meaning, "Is it a boy or a girl?"

"Hit's a bastard," answered the child simply.

While she is courting, a mountain girl will think a good deal about clothes. With native adaptability in turning her hand to anything, she is skillful in copying with materials she can afford the dresses she sees in catalogues and newspapers. But she must replenish her wardrobe often, for her laundering will not spare the fabric or color and her sewing is more for effect than durability. On Saturday afternoons and Sundays and at special gatherings she will make up her face liberally with all the cosmetics she can get. But when she meets the boy who inspired all this adornment she greets him indifferently. That is "manners."

Love is something to be taken seriously in the hills, and if an outsider is courting a mountain girl under the theory "love 'em and leave 'em," he would do well to leave promptly after she finds out about it. Recently an attractive outsider paid considerable attention to a mountain girl, expecting his work to take him elsewhere presently and terminate the affair. He made the mistake of inviting another girl to go for an automobile ride one night, just before he was planning to leave, and when he came home from his engagement, he found all the clothing he owned cut to ribbons.

Here is a story offered as gossip rather than history, that had its origin some years ago in one of the back coves.

THE COQUETTE

One soft June night Nettie Blaine rode in
To Otter Creek Valley to visit her kin.
Come up from the lowlands some distance away,
She planned to make a three months' stay
And avoid the worst of the steaming heat.
Her uncle, Joe Blaine, had ridden to meet
And bring her back from the nearest town.
He rode one horse and led one down.
Unused to riding, her bones felt unjointed.

When responsibility is put upon a mountain girl, she thriftily adapts herself to conditions

Joe's house was so small she was disappointed.
She liked the scenery thereabouts;
It was sweet and cool, but she had doubts
As to what she would do in the lonely place.
Wonder shadowed her pretty face.
Her eyes were blue-gray, wide and mild,
Her hair pale gold like an angel child,
Which she was not. That seraphic stare
Bespoke a soul that wasn't there.
Nettie was really a born coquette.
She might love some time. She hadn't yet.
Meantime she only played with men
And made some trouble now and then.
She loved attention. When she came
To the settlement it was just the same.
Men said of her beauty in less than a week,
"The handsomest girl the length of the Creek!"
From all her admirers she singled out two—
Young Troy McGirk, a comely man who
Was noted for prowess with women. Devotion
As fiery as Troy's was quite to her notion.
She wanted Waites Tracy. Troy wasn't enough.
Strange that she liked him, so bashful and rough,
Indifferent to women until he saw her.
She was just what he wanted. Well, such things occur.
The girl gave Wednesdays and Sundays to Troy,
But Tuesdays and Thursdays were Waites' to enjoy.
On the Creek it isn't the thing to do,
If you're "talkin' to" one to "talk to" two;
The place is too small for a girl to deal double.
She's sure to be caught and let in for trouble.
On Wednesday night Waites went to the store
Full of pleasant thoughts of the night before,
And on his way stopped in at the mill
To sit by the hopper and talk until
Old Uncle Freem had his corn meal ground,
And plenty of others were sitting around.

Large families take care of themselves, for there is always someone to look after the "least 'un"

Old Freem had worked on chairs that day.
He made a part of his living that way,
Turning the lathe with the water wheel
He used for grinding custom meal.
And someone said as they lounged about,
"Have you seen McGirk takin' Nettie out?
Wa'nt it fur them ye was turnin' chairs?
Are they settin' up fur themselves somewheres?"
Waites looked up and his face went white.
"McGirk and Nettie! That can't be right."
"Hit is. He sees her twice a week.
Hit's common talk along the Creek."
Waites went quietly out the door.
He didn't need to hear any more.
McGirk courting Nettie! He'd go and see.
Mounting he rode off rapidly.
So Troy McGirk splashed through the ford
And trotted under the laurel toward
The Blaines' log cabin where Nettie stayed
Just as Waites Tracy stopped in the shade
At the edge of the clearing and tied his horse,
Following Troy in his leisurely course.
He heard Nettie's voice as she called Troy's name
And the thrill in her tone was just the same
As it was last night when she greeted him.
He followed when the light grew dim
And they strolled around among the laurel.
He saw them kiss and heard them quarrel,
And what they said meant much to him.
He caught each word. His mouth was grim.
"I won't stand fur no other man, see!
When I got a girl, she belongs to me."
That was McGirk, and then Nettie said,
"Who's put ideas into your head?
There's only you. Don't scold me, dear!
If I didn't care, I wouldn't stay here."
"You let Tracy see you twice a week!"

"How can I help it? He stops to speak
A minute in passing with Uncle Joe."
Tracy knew all he wanted to know.
He stepped into view and drew his gun.
McGirk whipped out another one.
A moment thus. The tension mounted.
Every heart beat could be counted.
An answering look in the two men's eyes.
She had fooled them both with a passel of lies.
She screamed and backed against a tree.
Both men fired simultaneously.
And killed each other? I reckon not!
They stuck together. The girl was shot.

XII

New Cabins in the Laurel

After a boy and girl have been sparkin' long enough to know that they like each other, they are apt to skip away some day to Bakersville or maybe over the line into Tennessee and come home married. If they run away, they will try to keep the marriage secret as long as they can, even though there is no opposition from either family. Sometimes there is a wedding and then, in the back country, all the kinfolks will "set up to put the bride to bed."

The struggle for existence in the mountains is not too keen and a boy can afford to "keep up a wife" by the time he is nineteen or twenty. Marriage at sixteen or seventeen for girls is not uncommon. I know a girl married at eleven who had three children by the time she was seventeen. Another married at thirteen, had a baby when she was fourteen, and was divorced at fifteen, ready to start over again—but that is uncommon.

Marriages in the hills are no more and no less permanent than in other parts of the country, but sometimes in the back country there is no legal divorce between first and second unions. As one woman explained it, "If folks are poor and there ain't money to divorce, they just marry again anyhow if they want to." This short cut is in no way condoned by the community; it just happens.

*She adds soda according to some proportion of her own, and the result is the
whitest bread imaginable*

When the mountain girl marries and responsibility is put upon her, she thriftily adapts herself to conditions. A young girl of sixteen who was about to marry was looking at my wedding ring one day.

"Did you get that plain ring when you married?" she asked.

"Why, of course," I said, carelessly using a broad statement. "Everybody gets them then."

"Oh, no, they don't," she corrected me. "I ain't about to have one. I told Joe to spend his money for something we need. He's going to get me a dress."

"But I should think you'd want a wedding ring to keep always and so everybody will know you're married," I urged, pursuing the subject.

"Well, I won't need it for that," she said, with more logic than I had used. "Because all the folks we know will know about it just as soon as we marry, and hit'll be in the paper, and I don't see what difference hit would make to folks we don't know whether they can tell if I'm married or not, and anyhow, I'm not going anywhere but to Big Creek."

And she didn't have a ring, either.

The girl has probably made no preparations for her new home. Cannily, she gets her man first, knowing that until it actually happens, the marriage is uncertain. Anyway, there is no hurry about getting house-plunder, because while they figure things out they can live with one family or the other.

When he can, the husband will put up a little house of his own, thrown together of planed lumber with just enough underpinning to hold it up, either a bungalow of the simplest type or a hip-roofed, four-room cabin with an enveloping porch. The bride will get a stove, bed, and sheets, a few home-made chairs and a table, a range, and cooking utensils. Then she will sweep the yard, put out a garden and "pale" a few flowers in "brash" against the ravages of the dogs and chickens. If her man did not have a job when they married, he gets one now in one of the mines, or perhaps at one of the mica or spar grinding plants.

The wife will keep the little house clean without spending much time at it, boil the clothes in an iron kettle by the branch side, summer and winter; wash them in galvanized tubs and hang them on the fence; take care of the pigs and chickens; milk the cow and tend the garden. After the children come, they will all turn in and help, and there is not much lonely hoeing. She greatly prefers the out-door work. The mountain women are not at all the inarticulate, beaten-down drudges an outlander fancies them to be. He is apt to

Grandma Grindstaff of Beaver Creek is a practicing midwife at eighty-five

mistake reserve for inability at expression, and poised composure for leth-argy. There is nothing drab about a mountain woman when she knows you. The casual traveller, seeing a spare, tanned woman in old clothes, bending over a hoe in a cornfield so steep that she might fall the length of it, assumes that she is put upon, without considering what she herself thinks about it.

As summer advances, the beetles will make lace of the bean vines and leave rusty trails on the pods if she fails to pick them off or spray the plants. As vegetables and fruits mature, she dries apples, makes sauerkraut and pickled beans, and puts up dozens of jars of dewberries, cherries, peaches, apple butter, pickles, jelly, and preserves. Green beans strung through the middle and hung up to dry become haybeans, or leather breeches, which will later be cooked with fat-back like fresh beans. In the autumn, porch walls are full of them, as well as strings of sweet and hot peppers. The pig fattening in the pen will be shot when the weather turns cool enough in the fall, and the hams laid in salt to cure. Later they may be smoked over a hickory smudge, but more likely a last coating of salt and a dusting of pepper will finish them ready to cover and hang.

The mountain housewife sets a bountiful table. The cooking is old-fash-ioned and hearty, more Pennsylvania Dutch than southern except for the hot breads three times a day. She prepares a hot sauce for lettuce the same as it is made in Womelsdorf and Reading, and one can even get schnitz-und-knepps under a slightly different name, schnitz-and-buttons. A newcomer needs a little time to become accustomed to the mountain green-beans, which are fully developed pods with large beans inside, cooked for several hours and seasoned with fat-back. The more they are re-heated the better they taste.

The outsider will like the fried chicken and buttermilk biscuits that are served to him everywhere. Good soda biscuits have little in common with northern baking powder biscuits. The mixing and kneading are different. A mountain woman will invariably say, "I want my bread with soda. Baking powders (commonly used in the plural) hurt me if I eat 'em regular." And she will put flour into a wide flat pan, bury a spoonful of lard in the middle, pour in buttermilk until it looks right, and add soda according to some proportion of her own. Then she moistens the surrounding flour, working it into the center with her hands until enough dough is made up, and kneading it on a board with a folding motion, rolls the biscuits thin, and the result is the whitest bread imaginable with tender transverse flakes like puff-paste and just the right thickness to eat without splitting. The pastry of a mountain

Under a tree by the side of a branch an iron kettle steams over a pile of ashes

Pleasant mornings boiling the wash kettle by the branch side

woman's pie is more important than the filling. Fruit pies are spread especially thin, but there is a reason for making them that way. At church gatherings and reunions the pies from the different homes will be stacked one upon another and cut like a layer cake. The effect is a real pastry, something like a giant Napoleon.

Food is cheap in the hills, except the things that come in by truck. In 1929 when prices were at their height, a girl who worked for me told me that her sister set a good table for a family of seven without spending more than $10 a month in money at the store. Coffee, salt, spices, soda, baking powder, snuff, and tobacco are the principal things that must be bought. Snuff may be an important item in the monthly bill of a large family. A taste for snuff-dipping, once formed, is difficult to break, especially since many women begin as young children. The snuff is brushed on the gums inside the lower lip with a twig frayed out at one end and called a "tooth brush."

A body of superstitious lore colors hill living without dominating it as it once did. The mountain housewife conducts her gardening, housekeeping, and child-raising according to traditional rules designed to take advantage of the power of the moon and signs of the zodiac over growing things, and to propitiate the evil forces of sickness and death. She is careful to plant beans,

A battling stick is hard on the clothes, but it gets the dirt out

cucumbers, peas, and all top-bearing fruit when the sign of the zodiac is in the arms (the twins) so they will bear double; cabbage and lettuce and all kinds of greens when the sign is in the head. She chooses the time of dark nights when the sign is in the legs for potatoes and root crops. Corn should go in the ground when the dogwood whitens but the moon must be new so the corn will grow straight and tall. The moon also determines how many joints the cucumber vine will put forth before it flowers. If the seeds are planted three days after the new moon there will be but three joints before the blossom. Sprinkle fertilizer on the old of the moon so it will go down.

The time to kill pork is either three days before or three days after the moon turns. If you wait more than three days after the new moon, the meat will puff up as the moon swells. The grease will all fry out, if you kill the hog on too old a moon. Be careful not to pity the animal at the butchering or it will take longer to die.

It is risky to transplant a pine tree. If it lives the omen is good, but if it dies, it takes a member of the family with it. Never let a lilac bush grow tall enough to shade a grave or Death will come and fill it. If a hen crows instead of cackling, it means that one of the household will die. The worst thing you can do to beckon bad luck is to turn a chair on one leg. To carry a hoe through the house is almost as bad. Be careful never to step to the ground with one shoe on and one shoe off, because for each step you take you will pay with a day of bad luck. If you step over anyone it is an evil omen, but you can take the curse off by stepping back in your tracks.

The old shoes and stockings lying loose in the leaves near mountain cabins were not stranded there through carelessness. It would be bad luck to burn them or destroy them unnaturally because then the part of the body covered by the discarded garment would be burned. If a baby's dress is scorched in ironing, it may call fire to burn her in a spot just as big as the discolored place. In case of a burn from any cause, certain gifted old women know how to "talk the fire out."

The housekeeper of the back coves may not entirely believe in charms, but she will be careful not to fly in the face of fortune by flouting them. She knows about the girl who laughed when an old woman was charming a wart off her finger and was punished by having two hundred warts grow where one grew before. She did not get rid of them either until her sweetheart cut a buckeye stick that grew the same year, notched it once for each wart, and had her put a drop of blood from each in its proper notch. Then he carried away the stick and buried it in a place she would never see. When the stick rotted, the warts left. The hill woman knows people who cured warts by planting beans where the eaves fell, so deep they could never sprout, or by burying a stolen dish cloth. Her neighbors have taken their children to an old man up Beaver Creek to have him blow down their throats to cure thrash. His healing power is due to his being the seventh son. A seventh sister, a child who never saw his father's face, or a woman who married without changing her name has the same gift to banish thrash. It may also be cured by letting a child drink from a stranger's shoe.

If a baby is slow about cutting teeth, rub a minnow through its mouth. A mother can help her child to learn to walk by standing it behind the door and sweeping its dress with a broom for nine mornings.

Charms have especial power over blood. In case of hemorrhage in childbirth, the midwife may stop the flow by scraping an old felt hat. Norma Grindstaff's aunt could stop bleeding by reading a verse from the Bible without seeing the sick person. In case of blood poison put sugar on a yarn sock and set it afire. Then cut the poisoned part of the body a little and hold it over the blaze so the bad blood can run out. The same treatment will stop pain if you run a nail in your foot.

In brewing medicines, look for an herb the same shape as the organ you want to cure. Some of the wise women of the past generation achieved local fame as healers with potions. Norma Grindstaff remembers that among other ingredients Grandma McClellan used to use galax, ginseng, heart leaves, boneset, walnut bark, hog lard, mutton tallow, beef tallow, and beeswax for her healing drafts. The old lady used to give the children lists of herbs to hunt that kept them busy days on end. Most mountain women, brought up on the tradition of herb doctoring, have a wide knowledge of the plant life of their woods. Ever since they learned to turn ginseng into money back in the days of André Michaux's visit to the Blue Ridge, they have had sharp eyes for salable roots, herbs, and leaves.

Before the country opened up, home doctoring was necessary because physicians were few and travelling difficult. Thirty years ago the death rate among women in the Toe River country was shockingly high. Most of the activity in ridding the valley of childbed fever was the work of Miss Lydia Holman, a Spanish American War nurse, who came into the district shortly after 1900 and established the first nursing service. She came down the old road from Marion to the English Inn, forded the North Toe River in flood, and went to Ledger to care for Mrs. J. J. Ervine, the president of Wellesley College, who was desperately ill at her summer home there. Miss Holman has never gone back north to stay. When her patient was better, she rode alone all up and down the country wherever there was a sick call. At first she lived with Mrs. Ervine in the big frame house on the wooded bank above the Ledger-Bakersville road. Later, when her friend decided to sell the property, Miss Holman bought it and for ten years she lived there alone—when she found time to come home, sleep, and get fresh clothing before starting on a new case.

The work begun thus informally eventually received recognition. Fourteen years ago, with backing from friends in the north, she established the Holman Infirmary on a hill top at Altapass, four miles from Spruce Pine, on land given for the purpose by the Carolina, Clinchfield and Ohio Railroad. The Infirmary accommodates ten beds, and is designed primarily for mothers and babies. In 1934 Miss Holman had assisted at the birth of more than six hundred infants.

The McBee Clinic at Bakersville was opened in 1933. Besides these two Toe Valley foundations, there are hospitals easily accessible at Crossnore in the Linville country, and at Banner Elk in the Watauga section.

CHAPTER

XIII

Blockade

Liquor in the Toe River Valley is taken as a matter of course. There is plenty of corn whiskey and some of the fruit brandies, but there is also a lack of hysteria about it. "There always was blockade and hit's here yet." The hill man knows that he cannot drink it all and he does not try. There is more steady drinking than spree drinking. It is the visiting northerner who makes the worst exhibition on corn.

Whether the country as a whole is dry or wet makes very little difference to personal drinking habits in the Toe River country. Revenuers or prohibition officers look very much alike to the hill people. In the repeal election, however, the district voted overwhelmingly dry. In addition to a large religious group opposed to liquor, there was another faction which had discovered that the federal government, under the Eighteenth Amendment, was too busy to ferret out isolated stills. Toe River could produce more blockade and be sure of a market for it. Bakersville voted 535 dry against 22 wet; Cane Creek 311 dry to 7 wet; Grassy Creek Township, which includes the village of Spruce Pine, 804 dry to 132 wet; Herrel Township, covering the Big Rock Creek section, 283 dry to 25 wet; and Little Rock Creek 110 dry to 7 wet.

"There always was blockade, and it's here yet"

The quality of Toe River corn whiskey is good, although sometimes the distiller puts in too much lye to hurry up his mash or works off a run in an oil drum and taints it. None of it is aged very long, but some of the higher alcohols and impurities can be eliminated by putting a charred oak stick in a half-gallon fruit jar of the liquor. Charred peaches will serve the same purpose. Good straight-run corn is the most popular, and apple and blackberry brandy are the choicest and hardest to get. Third run sugar liquor is the meanest.

The commonest test for quality is to shake the jar and watch the bead that forms. If it holds without breaking and if the liquid climbs up the glass a little, it is good and there is not much water. Most of the stills are run by people who have been making blockade for years and are proud of their product as good housewives are proud of the flavor of their butter. People come to expect certain qualities in the liquor from certain stills. "That's some of the ole popscull from Deer Mountain," "That's some of Uncle Tate's first-run sweet mash," or "That's scorched sugar liquor from Owl Creek."

Medium quality straight-run corn may be had for $3 a gallon if the source is sure of you. It may be picked up at random for from fifty to seventy-five cents a short pint. Apple brandy is from five to seven dollars a gallon. In spite of the nation-wide reputation of the hill country for running "corn," the price is higher and there is probably less manufactured than in the cypress swamps on the coast where it may be bought for $1 a gallon, or $5 to $8 for a case of twelve half-gallons.

The trading in blockade in the Toe River Valley is neither flagrant nor defiant, but it goes on steadily even though the court is generally strict with offenders brought under its jurisdiction. It has been said that it is easier to get out of a murder charge in North Carolina than a liquor case. And yet the court can be kindly. An old man was brought before the judge not long ago for having two pints of liquor in his possession. When the judge asked him where he got the whiskey, he raised his right hand and said, "I swore I'd tell you the truth, judge, and I'm agoing to, and I swore to the fellow that I got it from that I wouldn't tell on him and I ain't *about* to. I won't tell you a lie, judge, but I kaint tell you the name neither."

The judge let it pass. Presently in the course of his questioning he asked, "If I let you go, uncle, what'll you do then?"

Up went the old man's right hand again as in taking oath. "If I got to tell the truth, judge, I swear to you I'll have to hunt me some more liquor for my old lady. She's got lots of ailments."

The Law was lenient.

"All right, uncle," ruled the judge. "Go home this time and get the liquor for your old lady, but see to it you don't ever get down here again."

Uncle Zack McHone enjoys the distinction of being the first man indicted for stilling and selling in Mitchell County.

"I got married in '67 to Ann Liza Dixon," he says, "and I got to studying how to get hold of some money. I could see that now when I was married I had to have it. Hit seemed like stillin' would be about the best I could do, so I rigged me out an outfit. I didn't think I was breakin' the law because there wa'n't no law, not for five years after the war there wa'n't.

"Then after awhile talk riz about a Revenue and sure enough they come on me, just as I was workin' in a place I'd picked below the house, and carried me down to Raleigh to be tried. Hit was Ed Ray (that killed Horton later) that took me. Him and Doc Lever. When I got there I thought they'd put me in a jail house. I saw the men going in the door in a jumble and I started right along with 'em. But Ed Ray clipped me on the shoulder and he says, 'Hi, where you goin'?'

"And I says, 'In the prison I suppose.'

"But he says, 'No, you haint. You're goin' with us.'

"So I stayed at a hotel and paid two dollars and a half a day for three weeks. Seems like I always had good friends. If there's a body in Mitchell, or Yancey, or Avery, or Tennessee either, that's my enemy, I don't know it. They let me go home, but in six months I had to go to Raleigh again. That time Lawyer Wood Flemon said for me to go home and he'd fight the case. Hit cost me pretty near three hundred dollars to get shet of that trouble, when dollars was dollars. I always liked the Flemons. One of my sons is named for Wood Flemon."

In the days when Uncle Rube Mosley was a deputy he assumed that inasmuch as the Law was something everybody had to put up with, he might as well be on the right side as on the wrong side. He managed nicely to be on both.

"I was deputized by the government for eighteen years to arrest people," he says, "and never but once did I tie my prisoners. That time was when I caught Birchfield and Hughes for messing with whiskey on Bowlen's Creek, but I untied 'em before I got 'em to town. I says to them reasonable, 'I don't like to

The quality of Toe River corn whiskey is good, although sometimes the distiller puts in too much lye to hurry up his mash

tie men up like mules and horses and I'll take the rope off you two if you won't cause me to go to shootin'.' They promised to come in peaceable and they did too.

"I was a whiskey peddler myself and I had to arrest the whiskey peddlers, but I never molested any but the bad ones that was causing trouble. I didn't want more than two men to back me up when I went for a fellow and plenty of the time I went out alone.

"There was a ninety cent government tax on legitimate whiskey and the usual price was $2.10 a gallon. Blockade was cheaper. I always gave a gallon of whiskey for a bushel of corn. You could make good whiskey for fifty cents a gallon if you didn't pay the tax. I gave up dealing with liquor though after a while. Pap got after me to quit and he kept telling me the time would come when men wouldn't put up with me no more. I argued like I wouldn't quit, but I did."

L. H. Wright was in office as chief of police for Spruce Pine during the thirteen years prior to 1933, a period when it took courage and quick wits to survive on the job. He is a remarkable shot and accustomed to being in tight places—a heavy-shouldered, quiet-mannered man of medium height, slightly stooped, with thick black hair and flowing mustache. He believes that the mountain people are running less and less liquor and he knows that they carry fewer guns. It used to be that whenever he made an arrest he had to take a pistol from his prisoner. Now it has been four years since he has had to disarm a man.

The worst encounter that he remembers was a gun fight alone against three whiskey peddlers in the lumber yard near the Altapass road by the bend in the river. The men had come in on the afternoon train with suitcases of liquor, and settled on the lumber yard as a good place to receive trade. Chief Wright took a deputy and went after them, but before he started, he changed his familiar hat and overcoat. By the time he had sighted them and jockeyed about for the best side from which to approach, he had become separated from the deputy and could not call to him without disclosing his position. As he came up in the darkness, a man was buying liquor, and the strangers assumed that Chief Wright was coming for the same thing. When he reached them he said, without drawing a gun, "You boys consider yourselves under arrest." At that, the customer ran, and the chief turned his head momentarily to call him to halt. It took no more than a second, but when he turned back to the strangers they had three guns leveled at him. They were standing a few feet apart on the slope above him; his own gun was in his pocket. If he put his hands up as they were telling him to do, they would probably kill him outright, as soon as they stripped him of his gun, to make sure that he did not identify them. If he tried to get his gun, he ran a good chance of being shot in the attempt to reach for it. Either way, it was bad business. He decided not to give up until he had to. Backing away a little as though frightened by their guns, he managed to turn sideways long enough to slip his hand into his pistol pocket. It turned out that he was quicker at shooting than they, but he was only one against three. Some eighteen shots were fired, and the flashes among the lumber piles lighted up the dark. One of the liquor men got a bullet in the shoulder, fell down the railroad embankment, and escaped. Later he was caught and sent to the chain gang for six years. One fled in the dark, and one lay on the ground with a bullet through his liver. He was kept in Spruce Pine three months under guard to recover from his wounds. At first he was detained in Tom English's old store building. Later he escaped, after he had been moved to a shack by the fair-grounds. He was captured, but the chief waived the charges because the man had suffered so much.

Blockade may complicate business deals in the Valley in a surprising way. The scene of the following conversation is a garage in Spruce Pine.*

"Bill Garvey's wife sure was mad at him this week, and you couldn't blame her."

"What's he done this time?"

"Oh, just something about a car deal. It won't hurt to tell, I guess, because he tells it on himself. You see he had a prospect for a new Chevie up Bald Creek, a fellow that could buy one and pay cash for it. He went up a time or two but didn't get anywhere. Just talked. And then he says, 'I got to thinking. That fellow used to like his liquor, but then when he got married, he sobered up and they appointed him deputy sheriff. I'd heard he hadn't drunk a drop in ten years, but I just figured he *might*.'

"Of course Bill knew it was risky business to offer him anything because, with him a deputy, hit might get him in trouble, but he just took some along with him in case he should want it. And he got Columbus Barnes to go with him to see if he couldn't close the deal and sell the car.

"Well, Bill was telling me they got hold of some apple brandy that was the finest there ever was. It would just stick to the jar, and smooth—it was velvet. But they couldn't get much, so they got some corn to go with it. It was mean old sugar liquor but it was all they could get right off. They thought maybe they had better keep the brandy for the prospect (maybe you know him, it was old Abe McClung), and they drunk some of the mean liquor themselves on the way up. They didn't drink only just a little snort either, according to Bill, but that stuff sneaks up on you.

"When they got there they talked to Abe awhile, but he wouldn't pin himself down to nothing, and Bill thought he'd try the brandy. He and Columbus started down to the car like they were going, and when they got a ways from the house Bill said:

"'I know you're a deputy and maybe I'm a fool to offer you anything, but if you care for it, I could give you a snort of the finest apple brandy you ever tasted.'

*Fictitious names have been substituted throughout this episode.

"And Abe says, 'I don't follow drinkin' any more but I'll try some.'

"So they went out and set down on the corn cob pile. Bill gave him some of the brandy, and they both had some with him (and they already had the returns on the corn they had drunk on the way up). They kept passing it back and forth. They never did get anything definite out of old Abe, though, as to whether he'd take the car or not. So they got in their car after a while and drove off, and when Bill came in his own yard and Dacie saw him she says, 'What on earth have you brought home, Bill Garvey?'

"And I swear he had the whole back seat of the car full of ducks and turkeys and chickens, and they were all flapping and flying. Abe had sold him everything movable on the place, and he hadn't sold Abe a thing. The next day when he went back to see if he couldn't close the car deal, Abe asked him if he'd come for his hog. He'd bought that, too.

"That wasn't the worst of it. Old Abe had gone over to Elizabethton in the meantime and bought him a car and paid cash for it after all their trouble. Abe McClung's a mean man to deal with, all right."

Doc Hoppas of Brushy Creek tells this story of how corn whiskey delayed the progress of the arbiters in a land survey dispute. I have taken the liberty of putting Doc's prose into the verse of the country.

BLOCKADE

The Long Road to Piny Cove

The sourwood boughs made a thin green screen.
The slender dogwood laced between
And kept out the sun, but the simmering heat
Oozed through softly, summer sweet,
And young Rafe Belfield lounged in his saddle
His shirt undone, long legs astraddle
And dangling down almost to the ground,
The little mare mincing and picking around.
He stared out beyond with half-shut eyes
Where the open gap of Lick Creek lies
And reckoned whether he'd get clear through
By dinner time as he hoped to do.
Below, two men were starting to ride

Doc Hoppas sits on the porch, his banjo held carelessly on his lap

Up the trail he was on. He stared down and tried
To make out who it was. That's why he ran
Almost straight into a horse and man.
The road there was narrow, no more than a ditch.
The man pulled up short, cut his horse with the switch
And rode on around, barely glanced, and passed by.
"That's Gates, the surveyor. Couldn't he try
Fur something to say? I wonder how come
He's acting so feisty? He's pesterin' some."
It was something to think of. That was at noon.
The other two men would be coming up soon.
But they didn't show up. He went down alone,
And there at the bottom was Uncle Zack Stone
With faithful Deal Ransom, both sitting still
On the backs of their horses. "We're waitin' until
A feller can holp us," volunteered Deal.
"We want to get yander and both of us feel
We kaint never make it. You understand?
Hit's this yere liquor. Give me a hand!
I'd like to get down and stand up a spell.
You see, I kaint talk much. Zack better tell—"
"You fool! Stay where you are!" yells Zack.
"Lord knows, kaint nobody get you back.
Belfield, I'm mighty glad you've come.
We'd set so long, I'd worried some
For fear nobody's come this way.
We got to get some place today.
Deal, where is it we have to go?
You're goin', too. You ought to know."
"To Piny Cove, Zack. That's the place.
We got to get there. Hit's a case
We can't let nothin' stand in the way.
We got to check on Gates' survey."
"I met Gates yander on Razorback."
"We was together," said Uncle Zack.
"And then he says, 'I won't fool no more,'
And cussed us out and ripped and tore

And went by himself. We slowed him so
Stoppin' to drink when he wanted to go
Wherever we're goin'. I don't feel to hurry
And fetch up all lather. Taint like me to worry
But I do want to get there and speak for my man
While Deal talks for his'n, providin' he can."
"Belfield haint heard about that," broke in Deal.
"The Piny Cove Kirbys have figured to steal
About half the land that's the Allens' by right
And Kirby and Allen got into a fight.
The feller surveyin' the land that they stole
Got knocked out cold with his own measurin' pole.
Now they've got Gates to survey out the line
And I favor the Allens. They're good friends of mine."
"The Kirbys ain't callin' for more than what's theirs.
I'm goin' to watch Gates. Any time that he dares
To edge the line in where it oughtn't to run
I'll sure call a halt. I can handle a gun."
"Zack, don't talk so!" counseled Deal.
"We're peacemakers. You mustn't feel
Fur stirrin' up another row.
The reason that we're goin' now
Is that they've had one. We're to see
He runs that line—" "Ye don't need me,"
Rafe interrupted, "I've got to go.
My girl's got dinner down below.
I'm late right now. You'll be all right.
Go on. I'll watch you out of sight."
"Don't go, Rafe! You know Zack's old
And I got more than I can hold,
So much I kaint go up that grade.
There wa'n't no saddle ever made
Could keep me from slipping over the tail
The minute I hit a steep up trail.
I kaint look out fur Uncle now.
All by himself ye kaint tell how
Or where he'll want to head that mare,

*Celo Mountain was named for a Virginia outlaw who took refuge in a cave
on the mountain side*

And I kaint help him. I don't care
For me, but I am choice of Zack.
He come with me. I'll bring him back.
We got a sight of work to do.
Runnin' a line. Did I tell you—?"
"Yes. You did. I heard it all—"
"Quick there! Ransom's goin' to fall!"
Called Zack, aslant of his saddle bow,
Weaving dizzily to and fro.
"Just ride behind him up the hill.
Ye kaint desert us now until
Ye've leastways seen us up to the top.
That's far enough. And then we'll stop
And you go on where you're started to.
Hit's the only Christian thing to do."
"Deal!" yelled Rafe. "Drop that demi-john!

There's no more drinkin' goin' on
If I got to go to the top with y'all.
Look at ye now! All ready to fall
And fixin' this minute to lap up some more."
"All the more reason ye kaint go before
Ye got us well started." Deal clung to Rafe's arm.
"If your girl's a mite peevish—oh well, what's the harm?
Hit ain't such a lot, just missin' a meal.
Take some corn, feller. We've plenty!" said Deal.
"You bet I'll take it. All you've got.
Yours too, Zack. You'd better not
Drink any more till you sober a bit.
Come on! Hand it over. My horse carries it."
"Ye can carry the jugs but ye needn't think
We'll give them up without a drink."
That was Zack, and Deal agreed
One sup was all that either'd need.
They wouldn't want another drop.
They'd ride straight on and never stop.
And Rafe gave in. "Well, just one then.
Remember not to ask again."
"My jug is particular how I hold her."
Zack tossed it fondly on his shoulder
And drank a most prodigious swallow.
He looked at Deal. "Rafe thinks I'm hollow.
Say, boy, d'ye know—the more I pour
The less hit seems I had before?
I'm finished, Deal. Are you ready to ride?"
"Ready, Zack. I'm fortified."
Rafe slung the jugs on the little mare
And climbed up back of Ransom where
He could steer him best and hold him on.
The three toiled slowly up upon
The tedious winding mountain road
With Deal's horse bearing a double load.
They sweated and cursed and slipped and stumbled,
While Deal clutched the saddle bow and grumbled,

And Rafe kept urging his horse ahead
And holding Deal. "Well, boys," Zack said,
"I feel as high as a Georgia pine!
I'll leave you fellers run the line.
Let Belfield do it. I don't care.
I don't reckon I'll be there."
They reached the top. Rafe called a halt.
"Ye kaint leave now. Hit ain't my fault,"
Said Uncle Zack. "Hit's just the heat.
But if I'm goin' to keep my seat,
You're goin' to have to make a trade
And hold to me on this down grade.
I kaint ride down hill sober even.
Rafe, ye ain't so set on leavin'?"
"I kaint leave Deal, Zack. He's the worst.
I'll stay with him like we started first.
You just make up your mind to ride.
Bear down on your heels. You'll stay astride."
Rafe wondered when the day would end.
Zack rode obediently round a bend
And fell head first. He never stirred.
"Hit was Zack a fallin' that we heard."
Ransom groaned. "We might a known
He couldn't ride by himself alone.
No use to look. I know he's dead.
I hate that. He fell like lead."
"Hold tight, Deal, while I go and see
How much he's hurt." "No! Don't leave me!"
But Rafe had jumped down on the ground.
"Keep your head up, Deal. Don't move around!"
"Don't go, I tell you. Uncle's dead.
Didn't you hear him pitch on his head?
He was feared of that and now it's done.
Don't leave me now. I'm the only one."
But Rafe ran down the trail to Zack
Lying stretched flat on his back.
He seemed all right. His eyes were wide.

The snake man's cabin stands in a loop of the Marion road

"I'm killed!" he said. "I'm smashed inside."
Rafe looked him over. "Come along.
You're just high. There's nothing wrong."
"Don't tell me that. I guess I know
When I fall and kill myself. Rafe, you go
And see to Deal. Don't let him fall.
You kaint do nothin' for me at all."
From behind came a heavy bumping sound.
Somebody else had hit the ground.
A grit of gravel, a horse's squeal,
And Rafe ran up the road to Deal.
He was fast asleep right where he fell
And anybody could foretell
He'd be long gone; not a bit of use
Of Rafe expecting to get loose.
He'd have to watch. He didn't dare
Go off and leave that drunken pair.
He dragged Deal down where Uncle slept.

The sun went down. A cold draft kept
The laurel branches tossing about.
The two slept on. Thought Rafe, "I doubt
But both may have come sober now.
I'm going to wake them anyhow."
He called and shook. They wouldn't stir.
It seemed their sleep was heavier
Than any time since they passed out.
He couldn't start them down without
He packed them like a load of wood.
And then he thought, "Suppose I could
Affright them so they'd up and start!
I might pretend I had a cart
And rout them out to let me by."
He hid in the brush. "Hallo, Deal! Hi!
Hup, Zack! You two clar out of there!
I'm like to tromp ye down, I swear.
I got a team and a heavy load.
What air ye doin' blockin' the road?"
Then Deal woke up and tried to climb
Out of the way. "Hey! Give me time
To wake up Uncle. Zack! Scoot over!
Get out of the road and let that drover
That's yellin' yander drive on by."
Zack didn't move. "I'll have to try
A little mite more. Wake up! Hit's me.
Ye got to get up. Do ye want to be
Broke all to bits? He's a real nice man.
Leave him go by as quick as you can."
"Are ye gone?" called the drover. "Here I come!"
"Not yet we ain't. I've tried him some
But he kaint hear a word I say.
Hold on! We're goin' to get away!"
Zack wouldn't rouse. Deal said at last,
"I'll save myself then. Go on past!"
He sat up, whirled his legs around
And lay back down upon the ground—

Right where he was. "Be on your way.
I'm gone!" he shouted. "Come ahead!
Good-bye, Zack. You're good as dead!"
Then he begged, "Kaint ye go slow
And sort of fix to hit him low?
If his legs get broke, I know they'd mend—"
Then Rafe stopped trying to pretend
That he was the teamster any more.
The two lay just as they were before.
When the moon came up Zack set up straight.
"Wake up, Deal! Hit's awful late.
Hey, Rafe! What's become of you?
Where's our horses wandered to?"
And then, "I just remember now.
I haint no horse. I wonder how
We'll get along? Remember, Deal?
He broke his legs in the wagon wheel
The time that teamster made a fuss
Fur room to pass and crowded us."

CHAPTER

XIV

Saints of Holiness

It is eight o'clock on a June evening, with bright sunset streamers trailing over the sky from Celo and Bowlen's Pyramid. The Estatoe Valley, with its zig-zag thread of concrete road running from end to end like a neatly mended crack, is already thickly shadowed, but the windows of the Holiness Church on the raw terraced knoll beyond the dinky-line to Hoot Owl gives back the sunset colours with a flat scarlet brilliance. There are two or three cars parked in the small muddy lane below the church, with a group of men and half-grown boys in overalls loitering between them. Women carrying babies bundled in blankets, with older children trudging in a line behind; courting couples; young mountain girls giggling arm in arm; and sober men in overalls, climb the two flights of steps to the unpainted church and disappear inside. When "preachin' takes up" and the singing begins, the loiterers by the road move to the upper flight of steps.

A broad unpainted platform with a low railing occupies one end of the building with the pulpit facing the center aisle and a cottage organ against the west wall. The room is dimly lighted by a kerosene lamp on the organ and another on the pulpit, the broad surface of which bears the words T H E

CHURCH OF GOD in big black letters. A bank of seats at the back of the platform at right angles to the altar rail is reserved for the brother saints, and rows of seats immediately behind the pulpit and facing the audience are for the sister saints. The body of the church is filled with benches made of hewn slats with the sharp edge up. The backs of the benches tilt away from the spine uncomfortably, but the benches are easier to sit on than the plank seats that have no backs at all.

A song is in full swing with the choir leader pacing back and forth, beating time with his hymn book. Everyone knows the words and the tune by heart.

> The Church of God is right
> Praise the Lamb!
> The Devil knows it's right
> Praise the Lamb!

As the tune is repeated over and over with slight changes in the words, the women sway lightly with the beat; one of them begins to clap her hands. Long shadows dance on the bare rafters and the refrain grows louder and faster.

> The Church of God is right
> Praise the Lamb!

When the singers are satisfied, the pastor, a sallow, youngish man in a blue suit, who has been reading his Bible by the lamp on the pulpit, calls for a prayer, naming one of the brothers to lead. There is a moment of scraping and shuffling as the saints kneel. Then a fury of supplication shakes the building as the Sanctified shout for the Lord's attention. A man, bowed close to the altar rail, stretches his arms heavenward again and again, clutching the air as though he would pull down a blessing by force, while he prays in a loud voice that knots the veins in his neck. Out of the confusion there rises now and then a stray "Hallelujah!" "Lord Bless the Lamb!"; but the rest is unintelligible. The uproar stops as quickly as it began and the saints resume their benches.

The pastor has his Bible open to preach. He will say only the words that Jesus puts into his mouth, picking texts at random. Leaning close to the lamp he reads the parable of the wise and the foolish virgins. Then he expounds it, walking up and down the rostrum with the Bible in his hand.

The sinners will occupy the benches in the body of the church; the seats on the platform are for the Saints of Holiness

"They had no oil in their lamps—No, sir. They hadn't no oil. Their lamps were empty. Brother, sister! Is your lamp empty? Is your name put down in the Book of the Lamb because if it ain't you're going to hell and the day's coming when we kaint he'p you, no-way-whatever. The foolish virgins came with no oil. They hadn't any at all, in any-way-whatever—" As words flow to his tongue the meaning flows out of them. They come louder and faster without connection, rising on to a plane of undifferentiated sing-song. Suddenly he stops by the light and chooses another passage from the Bible whose open pages flutter as he tramps between the pulpit and the benches of the sister saints.

" 'Cast not thy pearls before swine,' he reads, 'lest they turn again and rend thee.' Yes, sir, my friends, there's plenty of folks that loves the world that'll turn on a Church of God preacher when he tries to give them the Words and give him an uncommonly answer. Now I'm not saying any of you folks are hogs and I don't want you to take it that way, any-way-whatever, but I'm telling you if you turn away the Blessing, when we meet up there your name won't be in the Lamb's Book. There's lots of folks that's made hogs of themselves drinking liquor and going after the pleasures of this world. Yes, sir, and they'll meet a little dog comin' down the street and 'much' him, and then treat the church of God preacher worse than a dog." Dogs and hogs become entangled as the confusion of syllables comes upon him.

A woman from the front row of the saints comes forward to the pulpit and breaks into the preacher's exhortation with a testimonial. "Glory to God— Bless the Lamb," she cries and begins to talk "in tongues," a sure indication that the Holy Ghost has descended. A black-bearded man in a blue work shirt succeeds her in the pulpit. He begs the sinners to "leave-go" their sins and come up and pray with the Saved. In his fervor he flails his arms and jumps to the altar rail, and his face is hidden in the shadows of the bare beams.

The pastor has noticed a woman weeping in the audience among the rows of stolid sinners. He points her out to two of the saints, who leave the platform to exhort her. When they bring her behind the rail in triumph, all the Saved kneel about her and pray. Women are shouting in her ears on both sides. Men work themselves into a frenzy until their arms and heads jerk uncontrollably. The sinner is having a hard time "to get across to Glory." She beats the rail hopelessly with her clenched fists while the kneeling women urge her to hold on till she comes through Sanctified. Suddenly she screams, leaps into the air and begins to dance, stamping hard with her heels, arms loosely curved above her head, eyes closed and head rolling. She runs into the wall. The nearest saint pulls her away and lets her start off again. As she stamps toward the pulpit, the pastor snatches the lamp and carries it to the organ. The congregation of the saints lets go in earnest, rivalling the ecstasy of the reclaimed sinner. One of them whirls her right arm around and around grotesquely, and a lean, tanned woman dances her hair down, all the time praising God for the Sanctified soul.

The service ends without an offering or a benediction, and the lamps are blown out. Outside it is cool, moonlit, and unbelievably quiet.

The Holiness sect is the noisiest and the smallest religious congregation on Toe River. Their exaggerated religious frenzies are not characteristic of the other local church services. The village congregations on Toe River, where the outside influence is strongest, are as conservative as small town worshippers anywhere, but some of the country churches deal in vigorous emotional excitement on occasion. Almost any religious gathering—a "decoration" or a funeral quite as much as a revival—offers an opportunity for the release of pent-up emotion.

Toe River people are inveterate church goers. Baptist meeting-houses outnumber the rest, but there is a scattering of other Protestant congregations. The denomination is only a surface variation of a startlingly real, soul-shaking faith. Educational requirements or special denominational training for the preacher in the old-fashioned mountain churches is negligible. When a man gets "a call to preach," he stops mining spar or cutting timber and studies his Bible. Being a preacher is not so much a profession attained as the use of special talent given by the Lord when he "called" the man to shepherd his flock.

Among the mountain people the national Memorial Day passes unnoticed. In its place each of the country churches has its own "decoration," when the congregation holds a memorial service for the dead. These individual services, in a long procession from late spring to midsummer, are a timely chance for wide inter-churchly visiting.

The "decoration" at the Bear Creek Baptist church near Ledger is the largest in Mitchell County, and draws attendance from Yancey, Avery, and McDowell as well. The church stands on an open knoll, its broad, pillared porch facing the burying ground. Beside it rises Chestnut Flat Mountain, with the spar dump of a mine cutting through the green trees in a white scar away up under the ridge. Sugar Tree Cove slides between it and the green undulations of the Bald (technically Big Yellow). The by-road to the church leads from the Spruce Pine-Ledger road through a pleasant grove where on Decoration Day cars of every size and age edge forward with wagons, horses, and mules to join the close huddle in the sunny yard between the church and the cemetery. Everyone wears his best clothes, and the women and children carry flowers—"ivy" (mountain laurel) and "red laurel" (red rhododendron) just breaking the tight bud, lemon lilies, sweet peas, every flower in bloom at the season, as well as a profusion of paper flowers in bright, wired wreaths. The cemetery is a blaze of color with nodding blossoms on the low mounds.

The memorial service takes place within a group of juniper trees in the center of the burial ground. The moderator conducts the formalities, which are simple, and the choir sings without accompaniment those stirring mountain hymns that urge forward with hurrying tempo until the audience is tense as a bow string. The service reaches its emotional peak in the personal

The Holiness sect is the noisiest congregation on the Toe River

The Bear Creek Baptist Church stands on an open knoll, its broad, pillared porch facing the burying ground

remembrances and testimonials that follow. As the congregation crowds about the central group conducting the service, the pastor nods to one of the older members of the faith who knows how to release the flood gates. Stepping into the center of the circle without embarrassment, he testifies of his experience with a sober dignity that gradually deepens in intensity as he speaks of those whom he has loved and seen carried to this very ground for burial. One man just past middle age, spare and fiery, spoke of "Little Bill," commencing, "Y'all remember Little Bill that's lying up yonder. He was a poor, frail tabernacle and all there is left of him is there on the knoll, but we don't forget him."

And before he was done, tears stood in my own eyes for the little tabernacle whom I had never seen.

After one of the songs a sturdy, florid man with white curly hair walked to the center of the circle. As he caught sight of an old lady in the crowd, he took a flower from his coat lapel, saying, "I see Aunt Tenny has come here today, and I know she's thinking about Uncle Hase that was a good husband and a good father, and we're all missing him this year. I just want someone to give her this flower to lay on his grave with my remembrance, and I know I'm speaking for a lot of us."

The posy was passed back through the listeners to the old wife, who accepted it with a nod of her head, the tears running down the wrinkles in her spare brown cheeks.

Among the mountain churches the singing conventions rotate like the "decorations," and offer each church a chance to show what a good choir it has recruited from the members of its congregation. Using hymnals with shaped notes, the choirs sing in competition without organ accompaniment, their choir leaders launching them into the hymns with a tuning fork. It is a great social occasion, lasting the whole day. Often the church that is entertaining serves a picnic dinner to all comers.

The Bear Creek church is as famous for its singing-conventions as for its "decorations." I remember an occasion when three hundred dinners were served. The body of the building was full of choirs. A stranger could not tell where one began and another left off, but the home folks knew well enough. The church windows stood open, and the music poured out to the listeners in the yard and on the wide porch. A long table extended more than the length of the building on the shady side, piled full of boxes and baskets. When noon came, the choir filed out into the sunlight. Mothers and daughters unpacked the lunch baskets, and people crowded up to the tables. Everyone seemed to know everyone else. Each of the families in the entertaining congregation had its own section of the common table, and there was much inviting of relatives and visitors from other parishes to help themselves to the platters of fried chicken and roast meat, soda biscuits, cold sweet potatoes, cake, pickles, canned peaches, and stacked pies. I belonged to none of the visiting congregations and I was kin to no one, but the mountain hospitality reached out to me. Four families invited me to join them. After dinner the choirs went back into the church and the singing began again. Talk and laughter in the churchyard died down to low-spoken comment, and the well-beloved hymns poured out again hour after hour.

A funeral is a favorable time to frighten sinners into repentance with a tangible object lesson of what they are coming to. If the preacher harrows the sorrowing kinfolks with the promise of Judgment and Wrath-to-come until they break into wild keening that sends shivers through the listeners, it is only what might be expected in bereavement, and likely to bring some sinner to his senses. The comforting of the mourners will come about naturally by the passage of time. At a recent funeral a young mountain man remarked, "If any old cooter gets to goin' on like that over me when I'm dead, damned if I don't come back and haunt him."

On Toe River religious considerations are apt to color almost any abstract explanation or opinion. Fate Conley was slowly starving with cancer of the stomach in his cabin on Conley Ridge, his features carved to the last refinement by pain. It was as though an actual physical struggle with death were going on in that room, and always, after the grapple, the victim courageously waved his tormentor away. When he died at last, Mrs. Coley Dixon said:

"They say Fate Conley was three days a dyin', but I figure they're mistaken. The nurse could a looked at him and said, 'He's a dyin'' and she not knowed what was goin' on inside. I tell you, the Lord's fair, and he wouldn't let as good a man as Fate Conley suffer like that. We just ain't got the straight of it."

One day Uncle Milt Pendley was walking along the Toe River bottom land to a cabin below Humpback where he wanted to inquire for a Billy Wiseman table. Suddenly he stooped to pick up a queer, ridged pebble. As he walked, he turned it over and over in his hand. At last he observed, "Hit looks like this rock growed and then hit stopped growin'. You know what I figure? Hit stopped when Christ was crucified."

Another time he said, "I've studied about it a sight to figure out why the Lord made so much ivy and laurel, and I used to hate it in my young days, and then I just thought maybe hit wa'n't for no purpose but to be beautiful and that would have to be enough. And I've seen hit holp the country too, just by being so perty. Hit brings folks, and this same land grew mica and spar."

With religion playing a large part in mountain consciousness, it is natural that it should color local legend and anecdote. Here is an episode that occurred when corn liquor and religion both got to working at the same time.

THE BAPTIZING

No liquor was coming to Banner Creek.
The stills were idle at least a week.
The federal men had made a raid
And quieted the moonshine trade.

That is, it suspended by common consent
Until the snooping officers went.
Now Uncle Zack Stone planned to keep a supply,
So that whatever happened, he wouldn't go dry.
The raid surprised him. This time he was caught
Without any corn when it couldn't be bought.
It was early December. The weather was cold.
It was half a day's ride to where corn was sold,
And Uncle Zack wearily went to the store
To canvass his friends just one time more.
He asked each one. Not a bit of use.
Whoever he met had a good excuse
Why he couldn't part with more than a drink
Till Zack was discouraged. He sat down to think
On a box by the fire. Deal Ransom came in,
Somewhat younger than Uncle, a big man but thin.
Zack asked him for liquor, and Ransom had none.
At least Zack wasn't the only one
To be caught bone dry with such a thirst.
They agreed this drouth was quite the worse
That Banner Creek had ever known.
"We got to get liquor!" said Uncle Zack Stone.
"There ain't a pint of corn in town
A man can get. We might go down
And load up in Shiloh with whiskey to last
Until this scare of the Law goes past.
There's plenty of corn at the licensed still."
Then Ransom said, "I s'pose I will.
Hit hurts to pay the distillery price,
But good strong liquor would sure taste nice."
They started at once. It was nine o'clock
When the two rode under the Raven Rock
And came on Honeywaites McQuade
Who was out in search of good blockade.
They told him their errand. "Say Honey, what's wrong,
When we go to Shiloh, if you come along?"
It didn't take Honeywaites long to decide,

On Decoration Day cars of every age and size edge forward along the by-road to the church

Reckless and thirsty. "I'm with you. Let's ride!"
They came into Shiloh just about noon,
And Zack said, "Let's start back as soon
As we get our stuff. If we stay here,
We'll ride in the dark, and this time o' year
The trail up Razorback ain't so good."
Deal agreed he thought they should.
When Honey heard what they were saying,
He begged, "Don't hurry. I'm for staying.
We don't get out such an awful lot—"
"You'll fool around and like as not
Get drunk and not get back no more
And land in the jail-house. Come before
You start to tap that demi-john.
Let's tie it up and we'll go on.
You can swing one jug on either side
Of the horse's neck and while we ride,
We can take a drink any time we please

A long table, extended more than the length of the building on the shady side, is piled full of boxes and baskets. Mothers and daughters unpack the lunch, and people crowd up to the tables

With a good supply right by our knees."
The boy gave in. They fixed the load,
Two jugs to a horse, and took the road,
Expecting to eat at somebody's shack
Along the road to Razorback.
The day was cold but the corn was good,
And all three men took more than they should.
They were getting high when they came in sight
Of a new log cabin. "Say, boys, we might
Get a bit to eat if we stop in there,"
Called Uncle Zack. "You all don't care
About goin' hungry clar to the top.
This here looks good to me. Let's stop!"
The party paused for one drink more
As a song poured out through the cabin door.
McQuade spoke up. "This here's my choice.
I like the sound of that woman's voice."
"Hit's a mournful piece," Uncle Zack objected.

"Hit's a hymn tune, ain't it? So that's expected,
And you was the one that said, 'Let's eat.'"
"That's right. I did. She does sing sweet."
The three rode up to the door and dismounted.
Their frequent drinks of corn accounted
For the shakiness of their descent.
The woman could give them dinner. She sent
The children flying to pick a hen,
And while she cooked, she sang again,
A good old evangelical song
That fairly swept the men along.
An empty stomach and too much corn
Is enough to make a man forlorn.
Verse after verse the song progressed.
Honey became more and more distressed,
And Ransom said to Uncle Zack,
"I hope we get that poor fool back.
He doesn't hold his liquor well.
If he starts shoutin', ye kaint tell
How fur he'll go." "Now boys," said Honey,
"I guess y'all will think it's funny
To see me here convinced of sin.
Listen to her and you'll join in!"
Said Zack, "The way that Waites takes on,
I feel for tippin' the demi-john."
Zack and Ransom went out in disgust
To drink more corn, but that was just
More whiskey than the pair could stand,
They played right in that woman's hand.
She saw with righteous mounting joy
Repentance working on the boy,
And bent her efforts on the men.
She warned and prayed and sang again.
At two, old Zack and Ransom doubted.
At three, they sang and wept and shouted.
They had religion. The day sped on.
The liquor went down in the demi-john.

There is much inviting of relatives and visitors from other parishes to help themselves to the platters of fried chicken and roast meat, cold sweet potatoes, cake, pickles, canned peaches, and stacked pies

It was four o'clock when they left the table,
Shaken and fumbling, hardly able
To tell which horse belonged to who,
But sure that Faith would see them through.
As Honeywaites wavered on ahead
Deal rode up close to Zack and said,
"We stood in his way a little while back,
And that was wicked, wa'n't it, Zack?
I've seen him get religion before
And every time it wa'n't no more
Than a rash, plumb gone in a couple of days.
We got to keep him in righteous ways.
Say, Honeywaites, you'd be surprised
How grand you'd feel if you're baptized."
"If I'd feel better, do it quick.
It must be sin makes me so sick!"

And Uncle said, "All right. Let's seek
To save his soul in Rebel's Creek.
We've got to cross it anyway."
"Hit's sort of cold to do today."
"The corn he's drunk will keep him warm,"
Old Zack replied. "There ain't no harm
In doing everything we can.
We know he's been a sinful man."
The creek was opportunely near,
Ice at the edges, the middle clear.
They drew up the horses. "Waites, jump down.
We'll hold you tight so you won't drown!"
" 'On Jordan's stormy banks we stand,' "
Sang Random loudly. "Catch his hand!"
"Just a minute, Deal! You begun too soon.
Let's start on something that I know the tune."
"Oh leave out the singin'. Zack, you tell
How Honeywaites wants to keep out of Hell."
"Here stands a wicked man!" Zack shouted,
"He's drunk a sight and cussed and doubted
And now he'd like to be right good
And get to Heaven if he could.
(I guess we've said now all we oughter.)
Ready now, Honeywaites! Jump in the water!"
The icy creek closed over his head.
They dragged him on the ice and said,
"Do you feel better now? Have you shed your sin?"
"I'm feared I still got it." "Then jump back in!"
The third time under Waites felt sure
The freezing water had worked a cure.
He was saved completely, sanctified.
"He's too hopeful!" Zack denied.
"That's just three times. He needs seven,
A Bible number to get to Heaven."
Four more times they shoved him in
To wash his extra load of sin.
When they pulled him out from his last immersion

They felt dead certain of conversion.
But Waites only shivered with nothing to say.
He could hardly ride when they started away.
It may be his sins were less than before
But he had pneumonia for six weeks or more.

CHAPTER

XV

Comedy and Tragedy
at Bakersville

The fall term of Mitchell Superior Court is in session in the gray stone building with the cupola that plumps down importantly in a friendly huddle of stores and frame houses at the intersection of the Cane Creek and Toecane roads. Behind it bulks the great blue mass of Roan Mountain, running evenly into the Grassy Bald. Knots of men crowd the sidewalks under the trees, overflow into the spaces between parked cars on the highway, and straggle up the courthouse steps. Inside, in the littered dusty hall, more men and a few women stand at the foot of the steep stairs that lead to the court room. At the far end of the hall a narrower, steeper stairway for court officials and prisoners leads to the area behind the bar.

The court room itself is jammed with a shifting crowd that keeps the back door swinging. It smells of people sweating in clothes that have hung about stuffy cabins through seasons of fryings and boilings, of tobacco, liniment, dust, coal smoke, and musty law books. The seats have been raised in ascending rows—an after-thought to the original plan of the court room—

but the aisles remain flat. Thus the approach to the bar is flanked on either side by descending grades. The seats are good places in which to rest until a case comes up, but that is all they are good for. In spite of the elevation one cannot see over the heads of the men crowded along the bar.

Judge Ferry* sits on a small rostrum partially let into an alcove backed with sectional bookcases, and the jury is at his left in a double row at right angles to the bar facing the lawyers' tables. The witness stand is a straight chair set against the wall between the judge and jury and adjoining the door that opens into the jury room. A circulating heater with a long wavering stove pipe stands to the right. A narrow door between the judge's platform and the stove is the official entrance for prisoners, deputies, witnesses, lawyers, and court officers. A number of spectators filter in that way, too. Prisoners and their attendant deputies sit with their backs to the audience in chairs along the bar-rail under the chaperonage of the high sheriff himself.

Judge Ferry is presiding at the trial of Abel Holly for smashing deputy-sheriff Troy Dunn's nose and cheek-bone with a jug, biting his ear off, and leaving him unconscious in the road, with a minor charge of possession of liquor. The scars are still fresh on Dunn's reconstructed face. The prisoner, tall, heavy shouldered, and a little bald, is unruffled as the proceedings go forward. He has been in court before for selling whiskey, but that is nothing to be ashamed of. Just his hard luck to be caught. He killed a man once, a long time ago, in Tennessee, but he did time for it and that is over and done with. His neighbors have no fault to find with him and he has done the best he could by his boy since his wife died. The thing he hates worst about going to jail is that he will not be able to pay the child's keep while he does time.

John B. Lynch, the solicitor, is an old hand at mountain trials, broad-shouldered, hard and vigorous, with a voice that carries above the crying of babies, the shuffling of feet, the creaking of chairs, and the eternal whispering of the crowd; his spectacles and the bald spot crowding down his black hair look like a disguise assumed for a more amiable occasion. He has arrived at the stage in the case where he can enjoy himself. All the necessary facts have been satisfactorily established for the state. He will have a go at Holly, and then the prosecution will rest.

Holly marches to the stand.

*Fictitious names have been substituted throughout this chapter.

The court house plumps down importantly in a friendly huddle of stores and frame houses at the intersection of the Cane Creek and Toecane roads

"Where did you get that liquor you had in the jug?" asks the solicitor, leaning back in his chair beside Attorney Jacobs, swinging a blackjack, part of the evidence, around and around his wrist.

No answer.

"Come on now. Tell the jury where you got that liquor."

"I bought it." The prisoner's mouth snaps to a straight line.

"Oh, you bought it. Sure you didn't make it? Who'd you buy it from?"

No answer.

"We want to know all about this. Tell the jury who you bought it from! Was it a woman?"

"No. Hit was a man."

"What was the man's name?"

The prisoner is silent and looks stubborn. Lynch knows he won't tell, but keeps on for fun.

"Don't you know his name?"

"No, sir."

"You went out looking for liquor, didn't you?"

"Yes, sir."

"But you didn't know you'd find it."

"No, sir."

"Where did you meet this man you didn't know that sold you the liquor?"

"On Rock Creek."

"Well, what part of Rock Creek?"

"Up in the woods."

"Where were the woods?"

"They're on a mountain."

"How come you were up in those woods?"

"Just walking around."

"I see. You just went up in those woods to see the scenery. That right?"

"Yes, sir."

"And to look at the trees?" The solicitor looks out of the window back of the jury lounging in their chairs and waves his arm expansively at the red and gold and purple hillside. "And you met a man you didn't know and he sold you some liquor?"

"Yes, sir."

"How did he look?"

No answer.

"Did he have a cap on?"

"No, sir."

"A hat?"

"No, sir."

"What did he have on?"

The prisoner grins slyly and looks at his knees. Silence.

"What were you going to do with that liquor when you got it?"

"I was going to sell it."

"Well, well. So you sell liquor, do you?"

"No, sir."

"I see. You were just starting to sell it."

"No, sir."

"Ever been in court before on a liquor charge?"

"Yes, sir."

"How long ago?"

"Eight years."

"And you haven't sold any since?"

"No, sir."

"But you were starting again. You got this liquor from a man that you didn't know when you were up in the woods looking at scenery. Looked just like any mountain, didn't it?"

"Reckon it did."

"And then you just made up your mind to start selling again. That right?"

"No, sir."

"So you sold this whiskey—"

"I didn't sell it. I was takin' hit to an old man that was sick."

"What was his name?"

No answer.

"Well, tell the jury what you did when you got your liquor?"

"I took off my belt and hung it this-a-way under one shoulder and fastened on the jug—"

"Just like a little boy carrying his book bag. This the belt?"

The solicitor tosses a belt lying in front of him across the table toward the prisoner.

"Yes, sir."

"Sure it isn't your boy's? It looks too small for you."

"I got heavier now."

"That belt won't go round you."

"Hit will, too."

"Put it on, then, and show the jury."

The prisoner does so. He also demonstrates how he carried the jug after he took it off.

"But how did you hold up your pants?"

"They just stayed up."

"I see. You tied on the jug—under your coat, wasn't it?"

"Yes, sir."

"And went down the road, holding up your pants."

The sheriff raps for order, but laughter trickles all over the jury.

"No, sir. My pants stayed up themselves."

"And then you went down and smashed Troy Dunn in the face with the jug?"

"No, sir. I hit him with his own billy."

"What did you do with the jug?"

"I set it down a ways back."

"But it was lying right there when the fight was over, wasn't it?"

"Yes, sir."

"So you hit Troy Dunn with his billy—"

"He hit me first. He grabbed holt like this and was goin' to search me and took me a lick—"

"And how many licks did you hit him?"

"I don't know."

"Hit him about fifty licks, didn't you?"

"I thought he was going to kill me and I grabbed his billy and hit him."

"You don't like sheriffs much, do you? Interfere with your liquor business."

"No, sir. Yes, sir. I got nothin' against 'em."

"You ever been in any other fights?"

"Yes, sir."

"But it was always the other fellow started it."

"No, sir."

"Oh, so you started some of the fights."

"I guess so."

"When was that? Tell us about some you started."

"I can't remember. It was when I was a little boy in school."

"Was that where you learned about fighting?"

Silence.

Troy Dunn sits behind the solicitor. He leans over now to whisper in his ear. The solicitor takes another tack.

"You cussed an old man out a while back, didn't you? Went in his house and called him all sorts of names when he was so old he couldn't defend himself."

Silence.

"You did, didn't you?"

"I cussed him."

"What did you cuss the old man for?"

"He took my money."

Dunn prompts the solicitor again.

"What did you slap that old woman for a few months ago?"

"She ain't old."

"Oh, she's a young one, then."

"No, sir."

"Well, how old is she?"

"About my age."

"What did you slap her for?"

"She took my money."

"Everybody picks on you, don't they? It's a shame how folks take your money. So you slapped her?"

"Yes, sir."

"Ever kill anybody?"

"No, sir."

"Didn't you get sent to the penitentiary in Tennessee for killing a man?"

"No, sir."

"Never heard of Fate Henderson?"

"No, sir."

The solicitor knows that the prisoner is lying, and the prisoner knows that he knows, but he stares, poker-faced. The prosecutor grins at him.

"Come down."

Holly leaves the chair by the judge and picks his way to a seat by the rail next to a deputy. He is not sorry for what he did to Troy Dunn. When a man keeps following him around and bearing down on him, he's going to do something about it. He could have said a lot more on his side but it just didn't come out.

When the judge sentenced him to serve two years on the road on the assault count, one year for transporting, and one year for possession (suspended), he accepts it philosophically.

The banks of seats in the court room have filled unusually early this spring morning. Jeter Purdy of Ivy Creek is being tried for the murder of Waites Stillwell twenty-nine years ago. The solemnity of the occasion dims the brightness of the day and makes irreverent, like laughing in church, the pleasant country noises that blow in at the open windows—chickens clucking in a pen on a sunny bank with the rooster shouting at them; someone sharpening a tool with a whetstone; the click-click of a hoe on stones. The room is already hot, but someone keeps chunking up the fire in the stove until it pours out a blast that makes cheeks burn and eyes smart.

A swinging bridge crosses Toe River, which is too broad for a foot-log and too deep for anyone to wade

The sympathy of the community is with the accused, and has been with him during the week he has been lodged in jail. There are romantic developments in the case, and everyone feels that Purdy is being tried out of his time. Most of the witnesses are dead, and two of the lawyers on the case had not been born when the crime was committed. Jeter Purdy killed Waites Stillwell in a fight at a sawmill on Ivy Creek twenty-nine years ago. Then he left the country. Murder in those days was no serious matter, especially when committed under sufficient provocation. Stillwell had apparently tried to seduce Purdy's young wife, Linny, and was disposed to boast about it. If the defendant had stood trial at the time, he would probably have come clear with the law, but there was the powerful and numerous Stillwell family to consider.

So Purdy took his gun and disappeared into the woods, turning up later in McAllister, Indian Territory. From there he went to Moberly, Missouri, and then to Centerville, Iowa. He was anxious to return for his wife, but his father, fearing the vengeance of the Stillwells, forestalled his coming by writing him that Linny was dead. Believing that he was a widower, Purdy married Clara Corwin at Centerville. When he left Harmon township in

The mountain wall lies directly ahead

1902, a fugitive from justice, Jeter Purdy did not know his ABC's, but some years later in the West his education had advanced to the point where he was a member of the school board. He became a road commissioner, justice of the peace, and even served on a murder jury. When his wife's health failed, he took her to the Ozarks, and they lived there for a year. Later they moved to Columbia, Missouri, where he operated a coal mine. He became a dignified, prosperous citizen.

When his sister was widowed, he undertook to help her and her son and daughter, and brought them to Columbia. But the son was unwilling to go to school. Purdy, with all the reverence for education natural to one who has learned by his own efforts and who realizes that education has brought him prosperity, was determined that the boy must have schooling whether he wanted it or not. He allowed the child to be turned over to the truant officer. And then the shadow that had hung over Purdy so many years lowered and engulfed him. The sister whom he had helped, angered by his interference with her son, reported to the authorities that Purdy was wanted for murder in North Carolina.

So after twenty-nine years of freedom, he has been brought to the Mitchell County jail and suddenly finds himself the unhappy possessor of two wives.

A cornfield is tilted against the sky

Linny Purdy has been down to Bakersville to see him and promises all the aid she can give. Clara Corwin Purdy has mortgaged the property he had given her to provide money for the lawyers. Apparently both women love him, and he loves them both—the bride of his young days on Ivy Creek, for whom he had killed a man, and the wife with whom he had lived the best years of his life. During the weeks he has awaited trial people about the county have been more concerned about the two wives than about the murder of twenty-nine years ago.

Folding chairs for the witnesses are being placed in a row at right angles to the judge's platform and are promptly filled with spectators. A deputy shoos the women to the chairs behind the stove and the men back to the body of the hall. There are no seats left, so they lean on the bar-rail. The judge comes in by the narrow door beside the rostrum, hangs up his hat on the wall behind his chair, and puts on his glasses. The clerk works his way down the center aisle, pulls the bellrope that hangs through the ceiling, and returning to the box, adjures all those wanting justice in the state of North Carolina to draw nigh to the bar. The solicitor and private prosecution counsel and the three defense attorneys take their places. Purdy is led in, a heavy-set man with iron gray hair, gray suit, and deathly pallor darkening to bluish rings under his eyes. Linny Purdy, gray-haired, tall, and blue-eyed, takes a chair beside him.

The trial begins with the testimony of witnesses; the jury was impaneled yesterday. Jonah Baker, an eye witness to the crime and an uncle of the dead man by marriage, is the first to testify for the state. He describes the scene at the sawmill on Pigeon Creek in Harmon township that early morning in 1902 when Waites Stillwell and Jeter Purdy took up the quarrel that ended Stillwell's life. When Purdy came up, Stillwell was sitting on the roller bed with a small crowd of men waiting for the mill to start. When the trouble started, he heard Stillwell call to the men. "Don't let him kill me, boys!" whereupon he and Mart Barber, since dead, separated them, but not until Purdy had cut three gashes in Stillwell's leg and severed an artery.

Laurie Stillwell, the murdered man's daughter, is the second witness to take the stand for the state. She admits that her father had been drinking the day before the murder, but did not think he was intoxicated that morning. Purdy was living at the time in a house owned by her father, nearby the Stillwell cabin, with the mill about a hundred yards distant. She says that her father sent over to the Purdy home early on the morning of the murder to borrow a cut of chewing tobacco. Purdy refused it and her father called from his porch, "If a horse pasture and a mare pasture haint worth a chew of tobacco, I'll turn them both out."

And Purdy shouted back, "If you do, I'll kill you before the sun goes down. It has been in me along time to do it."

Fearing trouble, she was in and out of the house up until the time of the murder, watching her father, who had gone over to the mill. After the quarrel she saw Purdy "cut him two licks" before two men pulled them apart, and she heard her father say, "Bury me on the hillside, boys, for Jete Purdy has killed me."

Subsequent testimony and questioning discloses, however, that Purdy was not using Stillwell's pasture for either horse or mare at the time; that he did not chew tobacco; and that Laurie Stillwell, who denied having heard the loud angry talk which preceded the cutting, could hardly have heard her father's last words at so great a distance, if it were established that he spoke them.

The state's last witness, Martha Stiles, who was a girl of fourteen at the time of the murder and had come down to the mill to see her sweetheart, swears that she saw Purdy grab Stillwell's leg and cut three licks with his

The outlander spends time converted into money; the mountain man spends time itself

knife. Except in the number of gashes she substantiates the daughter's story. Then the state rests. So far, the testimony has run smoothly. The solicitor has dealt gently with his witnesses and the defense attorneys have been courteous in cross-examination.

Then Purdy is called to speak in his own defense. The day before the murder he and Stillwell had started home together from the store, both of them riding Stillwell's horse. However, they parted company before they had gone far, after Stillwell had called Linny Purdy a fool and insinuated something about a quarrel he had had with her, of which Purdy knew nothing.

The next morning, when Purdy was on his porch, Stillwell came down to the fence, quarrelsome with liquor, and asked if Linny had told him what he tried to do the day before. By that time Linny had. Stillwell wanted to fight it out then and there, but Purdy told him to go back home. He didn't want to fight a drunken man. As for the entire chew-of-tobacco-and-mare-pasture episode, according to Purdy it never happened. After the cuss fight Stillwell went to the mill and Purdy started down the road to Barber's farm where he kept his horse. As he went by the mill, Stillwell was half reclining on a load of lumber. He called to Purdy and asked him if he would work for him that day.

Purdy said he couldn't. Stillwell hollered, "I suppose you are still mad about what happened between us this morning," and raising his foot, kicked Purdy in the mouth, knocked out a tooth, and sent him backwards about four feet. And so the quarrel was renewed in earnest.

The thread of the story has been continually broken by objections from the prosecution and spirited tilts between the opposing attorneys for the admission of telling bits of evidence. Everyone leans forward to listen—and then the judge holds up the proceedings to give the ladies time to leave the court room. Purdy must tell exactly what Stillwell said about making advances to Linny Purdy. The women sort themselves out of the crowd reluctantly and the sheriff herds them into the little room by the judge's rostrum, where he leaves them jammed in a huddle among old ladders, empty ballot boxes, and all the odds and ends of political paraphernalia—everything but chairs. Somebody thoughtfully leaves the door ajar, but the sheriff comes and shuts it. The hum of voices in the court room goes on and on. Tired of standing around, the women try to sit on the narrow window sills—all but Linny Purdy, who stares out of the window without blinking. After a long time chairs scrape in the adjoining room and there is a general confusion. One of the women looks out. The court is leaving for dinner, having completely forgotten to let them out of their pen. In the meantime they have missed all the testimony about the years Purdy spent in the West, which followed the brief scandalous bit they were not allowed to hear.

The solicitor cross-examines after lunch, ragging, contradicting, interrupting, and restating with confusing inclusions. Purdy's face is ghastly; his mouth twitches uncontrollably at intervals, but his answers are thoughtful, unhurried, and courteous. The solicitor wants to see exactly how the murder was committed. He climbs on the lawyer's table and asks the prisoner to put him in exactly the same position Stillwell had been in, confusing him as much as possible with the repeated question, "You say it was like this. Are you sure? Put me just the way Stillwell was."

"That is as near as I can make it," says the prisoner.

"I said 'just exactly,' not 'something like it,' " and so on for ten minutes until the audience commences to be restless. The solicitor feels it instantly and resumes the action.

"Now take this knife," he says, "and show me just how you did it."

Purdy, who has been badgered almost to the breaking point, raises the knife and brings it down sharply, so near that the solicitor jumps back a little. Everyone grins, even the prisoner.

Then begins a long encounter between the defendant and the solicitor, who is trying to trap Purdy into admitting that Stillwell's advances to Linny were not the real reason for the murder. The prisoner is tired; the meaning of words has become confused in the long-drawn-out discussion; and while the audience holds its breath, the prosecution elicits an admission from Purdy that he was not mad at Stillwell for his treatment of his wife. He just "wasn't pleased."

The prosecution has scored.

A trembling old man in neat black clothes, his head drawn over between his shoulders so that he can peer only upward, his face swollen and yellow with a wasting disease, has been sitting among the witnesses. Everyone speculates about him, until he is called to testify. He turns out to be the doctor who had examined the dead man as he lay in his cabin after the cutting so many years ago. He had found one wound only, two inches long and an inch and a half deep on the thigh, a gash that would not have been fatal if it had not cut an artery. His story tallies with that of Purdy, who said he struck but once, aiming at the body but striking Stillwell's leg as the man half rose, pulling his gun. If the audience thought the cross-examination of the old doctor would be lenient out of consideration for his frailty, they are disappointed. The prosecution harries him endlessly, breaking in on the weak old voice, making fun of his deformity, dragging out an admission that he takes dope. Just then the chief defense attorney interrupts to crave permission for the doctor to tell why he takes drugs. The simple answer quiets any further questioning on that subject. He has taken morphine under the doctor's orders when the pain of the disease that is bowing him together was so great that he could not endure it. The spirit in the court room is changing, growing quieter and distinctly angry. This is beginning to be too much like whipping a horse tied up short in a stall.

Then comes the high point of the defense. A surprise witness, a square, kind man in horn-rimmed spectacles, proves to have been at the mill when Stillwell was killed, although it was supposed that Baker, who testified for the state, was the only eyewitness still alive. Charles Marvin of Tennessee testifies that on the morning of the killing he had come early to the sawmill, intending to ask for a job. He saw Stillwell kick Purdy and then draw a gun. Purdy

"D'ye reckon we could save victuals if we all had our teeth pulled?"

had been whittling a stick and had a small penknife in his hand. When Marvin saw that trouble was in the wind, he turned his head.

"Why did you do that?" shouts the solicitor, expecting to surprise the answer, "Because I didn't want to see Purdy cut him." He gets a surprise himself.

Marvin answers, "Because I didn't want to see Stillwell shoot."

The answer falls like a bombshell in the tense court room. It lands splendidly with the jury. The solicitor is at a loss for words and lets it pass. The audience wants to clap but only whispers and shuffles. The solicitor tries to regain ground in the cross-examination. Marvin has plenty of sense, but he can not read or write. The prosecution sets out to discredit his testimony with the jury, not by bringing out the simple fact that he is illiterate, but by using his ignorance of figures to cast doubt on his intelligence. The solicitor tries to trip him with question after question that would puzzle anyone undergoing the strain of the witness stand, even if he knew his arithmetic. "How old were you in 1903? Oh, but you told me you were 18 years old when you came to North Carolina in 1899? Don't you know how old you are? Well, then, why did you tell me you were 25 years old in 1903 when you couldn't have been? Don't you tell the truth? What are you fingering that book for? What's the matter with your chin? What's wrong with your eyes? What do you wear those glasses for?"

The witness answers that he had had to wear them ever since he was kicked in the face by a mule some time before.

"And haven't you been very bright since? Can't you tell the truth since the mule kicked you? Don't your neighbors say you can't tell the truth?"

Then more of the baiting with figures. Eventually the defense attorney stops it with the suggestion that Marvin tell the jury just how much schooling he has had. The witness admits with simple mountain dignity that he has had none at all. When he was growing up there had been no opportunity. Most of the jury are farmers who know how hard it was to get schooling forty or fifty years ago in the hills. The solicitor is hurting his case. Plenty of people in the audience can read little or none at all, and not because they had not wanted to learn. They put themselves in Marvin's place. The patience of the court room is on short tether, and knowing the frail barrier between thought and action in the hills, one can only marvel at the stolid inheritance of respect for county law that keeps the smoking anger from crackling into flame under the steady fanning. But one black-browed man from Ivy Creek, called subsequently as a character witness, stares at the solicitor with a glare so belligerent that he treats him with careful respect, possibly sensing the whisper running along the aisles.

"He better go easy on that one or he'll call him out."

The court finally adjourns for the night after depositions from Iowa and Missouri have established the good character of the accused during the years he has spent in the West. Ten witnesses have testified to Purdy's high local standing, and that Stillwell was a dangerous man when under the influence of liquor. The solicitor shakes off his robes of violence and becomes the affable man he looks; he has pushed the state's case to the utmost and never once has he tangled himself in the toils he laid for the witnesses. He knows that his audience expects a dramatic prosecution and he gave it to them. The court room clears and the hotel porches fill.

One cloud hangs blackly over the case—Purdy's confused admission that anger at Stillwell's insults had not been the cause of the killing. If it had gone home to the jurors, now snugly locked up, he has destroyed the straightforward simple defense that would normally have acquitted him. It seems obvious that he did not realize the admission, clouded as it was by progressive re-statement, but the jury is problematical after the solicitor's long hammering.

The prosecution and the defense argue all the following day. The prosecutor fights with such intensity that when he leaves the room for a minute, it is like a door slammed shut on a red hot furnace. Late in the afternoon the judge delivers his charge and turns the case over to the jury at five o'clock. They file back exactly an hour and four minutes later with a verdict of *Not Guilty*. Pandemonium breaks loose, now that the tension is relaxed. The audience claps and stamps. Everyone congratulates everybody else. Linny Purdy thanks each of the jurors with tears running down her face. Only Purdy sits ghastly and unmoved, without change of expression. He rises at last to thank the jury, and his voice fails him because of the very stress of his emotion. Silently he shakes hands with each one.

Outside in the street everyone wants to congratulate him at once, slap him on the back, and welcome him home a free man. Purdy and Linny are escorted to the Roan Mountain Café in triumph for the first meal they have had together in thirty years. One more problem hangs over them, but just now freedom is enough.

After the excitement was over, in the privacy of their reunion Linny settled it. Of her own free will she gave up to the other wife, and not because she did not love the man for whom she had lived thirty years alone. The best part of his life had been spent with the other woman, and he belonged to her. So Linny Purdy went back to Ivy Creek alone.

XVI

Fireside Industries

The growing market for handmade goods in the world outside the mountains has provided a chance for Toe River women to earn money at home. It has been eleven years now since the revival of weaving in the hills surrounding Conley Ridge. That it is a thriving industry today is due to the energy and foresight of Lucy Morgan, who as a former principal of the Appalachian School, learned at first hand the needs of the mountain women, and was fired to do something for them, or better, to help them help themselves.

The Appalachian School buildings are scattered informally over the hilltop known as Conley Ridge, which juts into the river valley at Penland in a wooded promontory and runs back in a circular sweep past the foot of Art'ur's Knob, enclosing a shallow inner valley along whose sunny slopes extend thirty acres of orchards belonging to the school farm. The entire farm-holding embraces 224 acres with thirty acres under cultivation in corn and wheat, and three acres in gardens. The school is reached by a circuitous road up a steep grade hanging along a narrow shoulder with a magnificent prospect of the Cane River Mountains and the narrow Ledger Valley.

The main building, the most recent addition to the school, is built of

*The husbands of the weavers cut and hauled the logs from their own lands
for the cabin*

cement blocks. Flat-roofed, large, and solid, with wide porches, it stands in a
grove of trees at the top of the hill, across the lane from Ridgeway Hall, a
wooden building devoted to class rooms that faces the trees fringing the
central valley. Morgan Hall, with wide stone chimneys and a deep porch,
stands on the point of the promontory looking on the Penland Valley. From
the main building a road winds around the horseshoe curve of the ridge past
a log pottery, skirts the orchards, and leads to the log community weaving
cabin, the barns, and the gardens.

The Appalachian School is an elementary day and boarding school supported by the Episcopal church. Weaving and modeling are taught in addition to the regular grade subjects. The project was first called the Seven
Springs Farm School, back in 1910 when Wesley Conley opened a mountain
school on land given by Colonel Isaac Bailey of Penland. Conley, who was
one of a large family, had no opportunity for an education when he was a
child, because there were no school facilities within reach. The education

*Finally Mrs. Henry Willis, who lives in a cabin on the Wing road, promised to
learn how to weave*

which he finally acquired came as the result of determined effort in the face of
hard conditions, working some of the time for fifty cents a day in a cotton
mill.

When he finished school in the teachers' training class in Knoxville, Tennessee, he started a Faith Fund, designed to found a school in the mountains
that would help others who were having the same struggle for learning that
he had had. The school was started on Conley Ridge, with Wesley Conley
and his brother for teachers. After the tragic death of his brother a couple of
years later, he agreed to sell the land belonging to Seven Springs Farm School
to Bishop Horner. The Bishop was to continue the work, and already had a
man in mind to undertake the project—Rufus Morgan, who was just gradu-
ating from the General Theological Seminary in New York. After Bishop
Horner had bought the land, Morgan came to Conley Ridge in 1913 and
took charge of the Appalachian School, living first in a cabin on the hill
above the Millam house. He continued as principal until 1917, when funds
were exhausted and the work had to be temporarily discontinued.

After the World War Bishop Horner urged Miss Amy Burt, who had been
teaching in a western college, to come and reopen the school. She came with

Uncle Milt Pendley will not make a chair at all, because he doesn't "feel fur to make chairs."
He is interested in tables

one worker, arriving in May, 1919. Miss Lucy Morgan, sister of the founder, Rufus Morgan, arrived the following month. Miss Morgan, as she came and went in the homes of the neighbors, realized their need for money. She wanted to help them, and she knew that whatever they did to earn money must be done at home, for most of them were mothers of families. The work must also be easily portable, because at that time there was no good road on the mountain, and raw material must come and the finished product go out on a human back if a horse or mule were not available.

Weaving had formerly been common in the community, but was then almost forgotten. Aunt Suzie Phillips' loom was standing out in the yard for the hens to roost on. Aunt Cindy Norman's had been chopped up for firewood. Miss Lucy felt that a revival of the old, partially-remembered craft might be the answer to her problem. After much persuasion she secured permission from Henry Willis to take his daughter Bonnie to Berea College for further work. Miss Lucy decided she would stay with her charge long enough to learn how to weave, so she could teach the craft on Conley Ridge. When Miss Morgan returned, Miss Burt bought two looms for the project with money sent by a friend in the North.

The first problem was to find an adult weaver to be taught. New undertakings are not pounced upon in the hill country. Finally Mrs. Henry Willis, Bonnie's mother, who lives in a cabin on the Wing road, promised to learn if Miss Morgan would teach her. The school agreed to furnish the material and pay for her output by the yard.

On a clear October morning a wagon carrying Miss Lucy and one of the precious foot-power looms jolted down the washed and rutted ditch that served as the Wing road, and toiled up the long lower slopes of Art'ur's Knob, eased along the ridge above the railroad that skirts a bend in the North Toe, and dropped down into the pine-shadowed yard of the Willis cabin. Miss Morgan stayed three days, until Mrs. Willis had woven a few inches by herself. Then she left her to work alone. Some time later Henry Willis came along the ridge to the school with the weaving packed in sacks on his mule. The check he took back to his wife was for $23. Mrs. Willis says that every neighbor along the road knew the exact amount of the check before she did. The next morning people came asking for looms before Miss Lucy was awake, and there has never been any difficulty to find weavers since. She says the first thing the older women usually buy with their newly earned money is a set of false teeth.

Art'ur Woody has been making chairs for forty years

The mountain man seems able to adapt himself to any kind of work

When the women had been weaving two years, the cabin where Rufus Morgan had lived was turned over to them for a weaving center where they could come together for supplies and instruction. It was small and dark, and after two years in these cramped quarters the weavers determined to build their own weaving cabin. The husbands cut and hauled logs from their own lands and raised the new building, with a substantial stone chimney, and many windows that look down the Valley toward Mount Celo and the loftiest range of mountains east of the Mississippi.

A day or so after the occasion Miss Lucy met Fate Conley, who lived in the cove below the weaving cabin, a middle-aged man, tall and spare with iron-gray hair. He greeted her with, "That log raisin' cost me five dollars!"

She inquired in surprise how that could be.

"Wa'll I broke my plate."

Miss Lucy was puzzled over what he meant, knowing there was not a plate on the mountain worth five dollars. He went on to explain that he meant his false teeth.

"How did you do it?" she asked. "I supposed you kept those in your mouth."

Charlie Woody knows just how far from the floor the seat of a chair should be

"Some do," agreed Fate. "But I got in the habit of taking out my lower set. I studied a lot about those teeth and how sharp they was. Just like two knives. They hit pre-cisely together and they'd cut a piece of corn bread in two just as easy as if hit was a piece of cake. Seems like I used a sight o' chewin' tobacco lately, and I thought it was my teeth that kept cuttin' and bitin' together all the time. So I ain't been wearing my lower set. When I eat I put 'em in my mouth, and when I'm done—back in my pocket they go. And I don't use a third of the tobacco I did." His face was sober but there was a twinkle in his eye.

"I had my teeth in my pocket the day of the raisin' and all at once when I went to hoist on one of the big logs, they got between the end of it and a cake o' tobacco I had in my pocket and broke squar in two. So I wrote to the tooth-dentist over at Bakersville and asked him how much hit would be to fix 'em and he said five dollars. So I wropped 'em up in a five dollar bill and tied 'em up and sent 'em, and they ain't back yet."

During the conversation Coley Dixon came up, an elderly man who lives on a slope of Art'ur's Knob in a green-roofed cabin that faces a row of juniper trees and the whole panorama of mountains. At the end of the recital he asked, "I say, Fate, d'ye reckon we could save victuals if we all had our teeth pulled?"

Wednesday is weaving day and all day long, regardless of weather, the weavers laden with their bundles trudge along the Ridge. Sometimes there are all-day sessions, with lunch and hymn singing, and always it is a clearing house for the exchange of ideas and news. One would need to live in the stillness of the hills to know what the comradeship of weaving day means.

In the early days of the industry Miss Lucy and Miss Burt used to pack a cargo of weaving into the back of a Ford car and visit gift shops and resort hotels in search of a market. The problem that threatened the enterprise was not production but sales. Up to 1931 there were sixty-three weavers at work, with more women anxious to begin as soon as the demand warranted additional production. The depression crammed the big storage cupboards on either side of the fireplace in the community cabin full to overflowing with unsold coverlids, dress materials, linens, scarfs, blankets, rugs, and runners, woven in rainbow colors concocted from mountain herbs and roots. Even a sharp reduction in prices would not move them.

Miss Morgan determined to take a long chance that might set the idle looms to working again. The crowds at the Century of Progress in Chicago offered a market with ready money if she could only get the goods there to be sold. Even a little concession would cost a thousand dollars, but she was determined to get it from somewhere. Nobody believed it could be done, but it was—mostly in contributions of two, three, and five dollars, collected from anybody who could be interested in the project. The purchases of the crowds at the Fair swept away the storage stock and set the business humming steadily again.

Each summer for the past five years Edward Worst of Chicago, nationally-known weaving authority, has conducted a ten-day weaving institute at Penland which attracts students from Maine to California. Mr. Worst gives his services at the Penland Institute in the interest of the betterment of the craft. One has only to compare the Conley Ridge-Ledger-Wing community with other outlying districts to realize what the weaving women's earnings have been able to do in improvement of living conditions and education of children.

The handicraft department of the school has recently branched out into pewter beating and leather tooling for men, with a subsidiary enterprise in the Art'ur's Knob pottery, a log barn half-way around the loop on the road to

When George Queen wants money, he can always sell another basket

the weaving cabin where the potters turn out home designed tiles, colored plaques, and pottery.

The hooked rug fever has never seriously struck the Toe River country, although sometimes a mountain woman comes to town with a tow sack full of ingenious patterns in startling colors, made by hooking dyed rags into gunny sacking. She will sell them from house to house, taking clothes or shoes as part payment.

The vogue for handmade goods strongly marked with individuality provides Blue Ridge cabinet makers a steady market for their old-fashioned rugged furniture. Uncle Milt Pendley in his shop at Beaver Creek Bridge can sell more corner cupboards in fifty-year-old cherry and walnut than he could possibly make if he hurried, which he does not. He approaches his craft with eighteenth-century dignity. He will not make a chair at all because he doesn't "feel fur to make chairs. I've made plenty for twenty-five cents apiece in my lifetime and I won't make no more." That ends it. He made the curly-maple and walnut dresser with panelled sides and turned columns, and the spool-end bedsteads by the fireplace in his bedroom, but he has not been interested in beds of late. He enjoys corner cupboards and tables. The cupboards must be made exactly in the proportion he learned as a boy, with poplar for the back so the red ants won't cut it, shelves of chestnut "so hit'll smell sweet," and if the front is to be of walnut, there must be a strip of white walnut down either side to contrast with the dark wood and "show how perty they go together." Underneath the lower doors the wood is curved up so the broom can get under to clean easily; the top has two arched ornaments ending in rosettes which he calls tobacco worms.

For ordinary table legs he uses "muscle turning." As he explains it, "Those little turns are for the ankle, and here the muscle swells out like your leg, and these bigger ridges make the knee and hit's done." The finished table is expertly mortised and pinned, and solid enough to last forever, because it is part of his creed to use plenty of timber. He has known all his wood intimately at least half a century.

"That's a piece of walnut from a tree my uncle gave me. Hit shaded his corn and one day he says, 'Son, get it out of there and hit's yours.'"

And indicating a piece of squared walnut like a giant beam, "I paid twenty dollars in gold for that when I was a young man and I been studyin' what to do with it ever since."

He loves wood for its texture as a woman loves cloth. There was one tree felled in this country that was unlike any wood with which anyone was familiar. It belongs to the maple family but it is neither curled, nor burled, nor bird's eye. The finished wood is patterned like marble with the undulations in the grain so strongly marked that it seems the surface must be uneven.

Uncle Milt tried to buy the tree, but the owner would not sell, hoping to get a high price for it in an outside market. Meanwhile the bole lay on the ground and started to rot. No other buyer having appeared, Uncle Milt finally got it. He has mourned ever since the rotted wood that had to be thrown away and the long blue stains that run into the marble pattern like shadows. Every usable scrap of the "perty wood" is cherished, and no outsider could buy a piece of it. He made a table for each of his three married children, and the last pieces went into the top of a candle stand.

Uncle Milt learned to make furniture from John Pendley, his uncle, who learned from Billy Wiseman, the run-away apprentice who brought a tradition of fine furniture to the Valley at the last of the eighteenth century. John Pendley learned from him how to make "painter's" (panther's) leg tables, but apparently Old Billy failed to pass on the secret of the movable ball in the claw. At least John Pendley always carved the legs with the ball fixed. Later, when the young Milton was learning to work in woods, he paid his uncle four dollars for the walnut legs which he uses today for a pattern. That was a big price in 1872, in spite of the fact that John had carved on them for two weeks.

The procedure of acquiring a piece of furniture may be long and drawn out, but it is highly interesting to both parties. Recently a woman who had seen the Pendley table asked Uncle Milt if he would make one for her. He countered with the proposition that he would try to unearth one of the original Billy Wiseman tables, inasmuch as she set such store by old things. He combed the district, only to find that the one available table had been dragged across the floor so many times in the hundred years and more of its use that the ball grasped in the painter's claws had worn completely off.

Then Uncle Milt recollected that his uncle had been working on a set of painter's legs when he died. He tried to find them by asking at all the cabins of his kinfolks, and after he had supposedly found that they were washed down Beaver Creek in the Big Freshet, they were actually located in the

The mountain girl is skillful and can turn her hand to anything

There is nothing drab about a mountain woman

Hanging Rock Valley, having found their way there through some ramification of kinship. Several weeks passed in dickering to secure them, and then the problem arose of how to get them to Spruce Pine, there being no regular road into the Hanging Rock Valley at the point Uncle Milt wanted to reach. He asked some of his friends from the neighborhood to bring the legs when they came to town for supplies. Thereafter he sat by the bridge every Saturday to watch for their arrival. When they did not come on several successive Saturdays, he became tired of waiting. He asked a kinsman to go with him and in the summer heat, seventy-nine years old, he walked the twelve miles over the mountain himself and brought back the heavy carved legs.

Then the timber had to be selected for the rest of the table, a weightier job than it sounds. A piece of walnut aged sixty years in water—the inside of a mill flume—would do for one end. Then the whole pile of dusty walnut planks in the corner of the shop had to be turned over to find a piece of timber red-brown enough to match it on the other end. How long should it be to look right with the size of the legs? Whatever the customer answers will be wrong, but her presence in the shop is stimulating by way of audience. Uncle Milt loves to ask advice, for the sake of politeness, but he never takes it. And so on with innumerable conferences until the last wooden pin goes into place.

Uncle Milt is an expert at making wooden keelers, piggins, and buckets, the distinction being that a keeler is a wooden measure of peck size or less without a handle; a piggin has a straight handle on one side only, so that as it balances on the hip, the handle lies in the angle of the elbow; and the bucket has a complete bail. A pail is a measure over peck size with a handle like a bucket.

As yet there is little profiteering in woodcraft, and buying is along the simplest lines. The Woodys on Grassy Creek, who turn chairs on a lathe run by a water wheel when they are not grinding meal, will charge you at the same rate for one or two chairs as for ten, because they are all made as cheaply as it is possible to do it. Charlie Woody, the son, has been making chairs for twenty years. Art'ur, his father, has made them for forty. The grandfather, Henry Woody, made them before that, and so did the great-grandfather, Wyatt Woody, back in the days when John Strother was surveying the North Carolina-Tennessee line. The Woody chairs are fashioned in simple mountain style with comfortably curved two-slat backs; they make four-slat rockers, children's high chairs, low play-chairs, ladder-backs, and chairs with woven insets between the posts; all are bottomed with hickory bark or whiteoak splits. And out of the little mill come beds with hickory-bark head boards, cord bottom settees, hearth stools, stands with woven tops, trestle tables put together with wooden pins, everything according to the needs of the customer who fords the branch and comes in the sunny door of the little shop. If he is a tall man, Charlie knows just how far from the floor the chair seat must be. The two middle-aged sisters, maiden and very shy, who live with the father and mother in the house half-way up the slope where the corn field climbs the hill to the road, weave the bottoms and the backs.

If one walks down the slanting path to the angle of the weathered house, with its upstairs and downstairs porches running full length of the identical wings, he will leave behind the year and the date and pick a snatch from a leisurely time long gone. A gourd is drying on a rock in the shady angle; a bucket of cold water stands on a pile of new lumber against the porch wall; a coil of hickory bark trails half unwound by the kitchen door; honeysuckle, bleeding hearts, marigolds, and zinnias in clumps between the rocks have been "paled wi' brash" against the ravages of the chickens. The Valley branch bubbles below the house wall at the back. And Art'ur Woody, tall and ruddy in spite of his years, will tell you how he made his own foot lathe when he was old enough to start making chairs. He thinks water power is a great improvement, but he likes to remember that he could turn a chair in thirty minutes without it. In those days he could reach Marion in five hours on foot, which meant travelling nineteen miles over rough country.

The little box house contrived of odd lengths of lumber where Preacher Queen weaves his baskets overlooks the Plumtree road from the bank side at Ingalls. The title is honorary. He is a tiny old man, almost a dwarf, with a tremendous growth of whiskers, who assumes that everyone is deaf because he is. He supplies the countryside with white-oak-split baskets suited to fill any need; hip baskets flat on one side for carrying in the crotch of the elbow; baskets with melon bottoms in quart and peck sizes, handy for grain, or with flat bottoms for marketing. As a side line, he bottoms chairs. Life is very simple to Preacher Queen—a good God to look out for him and see that he gets two dollars every month for his house rent; grown sons who make up among themselves one of the best string bands in the Valley, and a very little wife who isn't afraid to work. Town people give him his clothes. When he wants money, he can always sell another basket.

XVII

The Mayland Fair

The Mayland Fair, held in September on a wooded knoll above Spruce Pine, belongs to the three counties of the Toe River Valley, Mitchell, Avery and Yancey, the first letters of whose names suggested the title. In common with other country fairs it offers midway attractions and fills the town with strangers come to sell to the crowd or to watch the crowd buy. There its likeness to other fairs ceases. It is a four-day mountain holiday that draws active participants from the remotest clearings. They make their own fair. The tinsel and ballyhoo of the travelling shows are of negligible importance to a people bent on entertaining themselves in their own way. It is a huge home talent play with everybody in it, doing the thing he enjoys most.

Rivalry is the mainspring of interest, with the worth of a prize second to the honor of winning it. Uncle Milt Pendley begins planning for the Fair in the early spring, and works for weeks on a piece of furniture to win a blue ribbon that carries with it a prize of two dollars. Private gem collections of local origin, cases of Indian relics, and rare minerals compete for honors. Local schools vie between departments for the best exhibits; farmers for the best all around vegetable and grain displays, and for pig, sheep, cattle and poultry awards; women for the best pies, canned goods, biscuits, cake, needlework, potted plants, and cut flowers. And oh, the heart burnings of the defeated! The feldspar, mica, and kaolin companies build elaborate booths in the main building to house their displays. At the Fair in 1932 one mineral exhibitor gave tiny garnets to the crowd from a box marked "Help Yourself."

Of late years the crowds have been peaceable and well behaved. Not a single arrest was made in 1932, in contrast to six years before, when Chief Wright remembers arresting forty and having the calaboose so full that some of the prisoners had to be herded outside and guarded separately.

There is a story of Fair time in the road construction period that will be remembered in September for years by those who knew Spruce Pine in the old days.

AN EPISODE

Along in September comes Toe River Fair.
Hit holds at Spruce Pine and seems like we care
A sight more for that than the rest of the year.
There's an Otter Creek man that works close to here
That's a plum fool for fairs. (You know Arley Ford?)
As soon as hit starts he's headin' toward
The place hit's at. This year he was sick
And couldn't get down town near so quick
As he wanted to. Hit fell this way.
He was feelin' sort of low one day
Just when the Doc was goin' by
And he thought maybe he'd better try
A few of his pills. (The Fair was so near
He was takin' no chances on gettin' down here.)
'Course he wanted to feel the best he could.
Well, the pills didn't work like he thought they would.
(I guess maybe he took too many
When he's no hand fur takin' any.)
They put him right down flat in bed,
And looked like he'd stay there instead
Of goin' to town. Well, Arley was mad,
Begrudgin' the time when he could a had
A lot of fun if he'd got to the Fair.
But the first of the week he didn't dare

In common with other country fairs, the Mayland Fair offers midway attractions, and fills the town with strangers come to sell to the crowd or to watch the crowd buy

Try to get up. When hit came to the last
And him in the bed and the Fair most past
He got up anyhow and went.
As soon as he got to town he spent
A little time to hunt McGown.
(He's the Doc who put him down.)
He knew he'd be in town, of course,
And pretty soon he saw his horse,
A rangy red and white piebald,
And Arley stepped in the road and called,
"Hey, Doc! I want to settle with you
For the pills I got. How much is due?"
"About two dollars," says McGown,
Pullin' over and lookin' down
Where Arley stood by the horse's head.
"Here's your money," Arley said.
"Now do I owe ye anything?"

The tinsel and ballyhoo of the travelling shows are of negligible importance to a people bent on entertaining themselves in their own way

"No," says the Doc. Ford makes a swing
At the horse with his hat. "Well, you owe me
A week in the bed. I'm collectin', see!"
And he slapped the horse again with his hat
So he danced and snorted. Did I say that
Old Doc McGown had a wooden leg?
You ought to have heard him holler and beg
With Arley holding the horse by the bridle
And makin' him lunge and rare up and sidle
While he led him down the length of the street,
And when the horse steadied a little he'd beat
Him again. "Ye old quack!" he'd say.
"I'll learn ye." At last folks pulled him away
And let the Doc go. Then he went for the Mayor
And got Arley arrested. He'd just reached the Fair
And was buyin' his ticket. He felt pretty bad
To be dragged back then right after he had

Missed so much already with stayin' in bed.
He begged them to fine him and loose him instead
Of shuttin' him up in the jail house alone.
But the Judge wouldn't do it. He said that he'd shown
He was like to make trouble. He'd loose him next day,
And he stuck to his text spite of all we could say.
(Plenty spoke for him.) Well, Chief locked him in
And there Arley sat. Hit looked like a sin
With the Fair goin' on and him penned inside
Fur no more than takin' the Doc fur a ride.
The jail house is somethin' the size of a coop.
There's one little window. We'd go up and stoop
And hear what it was that Arley was sayin'
In there all alone! Hit was killin' him stayin'.
He'd beg to get out. We'd go to the Mayor
And then to the Judge. "No! Arley stays there!"
Was all we could get. Hit was just about noon.
The Otter Creek men don't get down so soon
Into town as the rest. They live so fur out.
Right off when they came they asked all about
Who was up in the jail, and went up to look
Through the hole at Arley; and first peek they took
He began to cheer up and asked 'em first thing,
"Is Troy McGirk with you? Have somebody bring
Him where I can talk to him. He'll get me loose."
And we said to the Creek men, "Hit ain't any use.
We've seen the Judge and he says 'No.'"
"If he wants McGirk, we'll get him though.
Troy couldn't wait to get to the Fair
But any of us will fetch him from there."
Two or three of the men started off for McGirk
And the minute he heard it, he's startin' to work
To get Arley loose from the Law. To commence
He picked him a rail from the Fair Ground fence.
(Troy's a stout feller, the best lookin' one
Of Virgil McGirk's boys, and best with his gun.)
When he saw him comin', we knew what he'd do,

One day of the Fair belongs particularly to the local fox hunters, who conduct a bench show and a fox race started from the Fair Grounds in view of the crowd

And plenty of men would holp with it, too.
He pried underneath, got a holt fur his rail
And we all give a hand and tipped over the jail.
There wa'nt any floor, so Arley was out.
"Won't they catch him?" we asks. "No," Troy says, "I doubt
They'll have any place to keep him, and then
Supposin' they do, we'll loose him again."
The Judge had been workin' to please McGown,
But when he considered the Creek men in town
He let the thing drop. (He don't stand in their way.)
And Arley got loose with no fine to pay.

The musical contests between rival string bands, quartettes, choirs, and fiddlers of the three counties are continuous throughout the week. Amplified by the microphone on the wooden singing stand above the main exhibit building, where the contests are held, the music fills the Valley of the Toe to the opposite hillside. The listeners stand immobile under the trees hour after

Ordinarily the chase takes place at night, the hunters following the dogs on foot or sitting comfortably about a fire in the woods, with a jug close by, while the dogs run

hour and refuse to be distracted as the singers, with the detached manner that is as much a part of mountain music as the galloping regular beat, sing the songs that belong to the mountains.

A barker carrying a squawking chicken and a showman bearing a long curling snake above his head stumble along over the uneven ground in front of the grandstand in a ridiculous parade, a squad of small boys and two muddy long-skirted gypsy children tagging along at the end.

"Hear! Hear!" bawls the barker. "See the snake eat the chicken alive. Performance about to take place." The mountain people listening on the slope to Gus Washburn's string band are like trees through which a rude gust of wind blows. They bow with the breeze but remain rooted. The snake show will keep. Gus Washburn is playing a piece that somebody from McKinney Gap made up. Can't miss that. These songs spring from the lives of the listeners. They know all about the story chronicled by the song, whose version it is, and they know the singers.

The bank below the singing stand that overlooks the lane running from the grove on top of the hill to the midway will be jammed with mountain people as the time approaches for the steel drilling contests and the tug of

The struggle for existence in the mountains is not too keen

war between teams from the feldspar and mica companies. In 1927 Matt Cook, a woman miner, swung the sledge hammer for twenty minutes while her husband held the steel for her. The men contestants alternated and thus had rest periods, but not Matt.

One day belongs particularly to the local fox hunters, who conduct a bench show and fox race started from the Fair Grounds in view of the crowd. Mountain fox races do not feature horses as a part of the chase. For a good race, the actual capture of the fox is not necessary, hardly sporting. Except for exhibition purposes at the time of the Fair, the chase takes place at night, the hunters following the dogs on foot or sitting comfortably about a fire in the woods, with a jug close by, while the dogs run. The men know the country well enough to tell by the baying to what glen the fox has led the pack, and they enjoy picking out their own dogs' contribution to the music. Foxes appear to like being run. A district where fox hunting is lively has more and not fewer foxes to hunt.

In a Valley home the fox hound is a member of the family. As long as there is anything to eat, he will get his share. Recently a man was called before the judge at Bakersville for failing to pay a fine of several terms' standing. When the judge asked him why he kept evading the settlement, he said he had nothing he could turn into money. Pressed for further details, it appeared that all he had was his children and two fox hounds.

"Our solicitor here is quite a fox hunter," suggested the judge. "You might be able to make a deal with him for the dogs and then you wouldn't have to feed them."

"No, sir!" said the delinquent. "I'm feared he might talk hateful to them like he done to me. He kaint have 'em at all."

The last night of the Fair, which marks the withdrawal of the exhibits and the departure of the alien shows, is best of all on Toe River. Now that the serious business of rivalry is over and the prizes are awarded, there is nothing to do but play. Regardless of the long road home to a cabin on the far side of Yancey or Avery County, the hill folks stay late in a last burst of gayety, dancing on the little stand that held the musical contests all week, milling up and down the midway to watch the ferris wheel taken down and the Bingo pavilion dismantled. The woman who was buried alive has been dug up and is sitting on a pile of canvas talking to the Indian fortune teller. Anybody can look at the fat woman now without paying for it. The crowd eats up the last of the hot dogs; there is some drinking, a little fighting, and a lot of courting. Then the lights go out and the Fair is over.

CHAPTER

XVIII

"Black Jack Davie"

The importance accorded the string band and choir contests at the Mayland Fair is proportional to the part music plays in Toe River life. To a newcomer in the mountains it seems that an upsetting alien music is everywhere. He does not know how to react to its high, running tempo or head tones, but react he will with a lively enthusiasm or definite antipathy before he has been in the Valley long. The songs themselves are different, as well as the manner of singing. This is one of the last retreats of ballad and folk song.

Cecil Sharp said of his visit to this country sometime in 1915, "I found myself for the first time in my life in a community in which singing was as common and almost as universal a practice as speaking." Under modern conditions, the universality of singing remains the same, although there is a growing tendency to do it vicariously by listening to Victrola records, and the material is no longer purely traditional. The Spruce Pine music store is a popular place in which to wait for husbands and sweethearts and at the same time entertain oneself with the big collection of records. Mountain music issues from it all day long, "Omie Wise," "Kitty Wells," "The Forsaken Lover," "The Death of Floyd Collins," "Frankie Silvers," or the long, doleful "Old Smoky":

On top of old Smoky
All covered with snow
I lost my true lover
By courting too slow.

"Walkin' in the Parlor" and "Sally Goodin" are in merrier mood.

I had a piece of pie
And I had a piece of puddin'
I gave it all away
To hug Sally Goodin.

I went up on a hillside
Saw my Sally comin'.
Thought to my soul
I'd kill myself a runnin'.

In the hills the rhythm of the singing counts for more than the tone. The beat must be what the ear has been led to expect from the foregoing phrase. If a line of verse has come to have too many syllables to scan properly, it will be slurred to fit the rhythm somehow and the effect will not be faulty. When Doc Hoppas sings the "Rim Rock Ranch," the lines run thus:

Goodbye to my friends and re*la*tives
Goodbye to the girl that I love.

The rhythm satisfies the ear because he naturally puts the emphasis where it belongs, even though he must mispronounce a word in order for the line to scan as it should.

In spite of its title, which belongs to another locale, the "Rim Rock Ranch" is a good type of the new folk song of the mountains, besides being an illustration of the urge for rhythm that is part of the atmosphere. Doc Hoppas read a book called *The Rim Rock Ranch*. The dramatic qualities appealed to him, and he made it his own by translating it into the mountain mood; that is, he expressed his own reaction in rhythm. Thus we have a highland song with outlander material.

At this time the modern folk songs, especially those featuring yodelling, are most popular with the young people, but the love songs (the mountain name for ballads), never lose their popularity. Most of the young people can sing parts of some of the traditional English ballads or are at least familiar with them, but they are by no means so commonly known as when Cecil Sharp came to the mountains.

I. G. Greer, who is a native of the mountains, told me that when he was fourteen years old he could sing forty of the old songs. Such a repertoire would be unusual now. In the course of years of serious research Mr. Greer has been able to collect some three hundred ballads and folk songs in the mountains, but his sources have been mainly old people. He sings the songs in the traditional manner, his wife accompanying him on the dulcimer, a rare instrument these days. This is his text of "Black Jack Davie."

BLACK JACK DAVIE

Black Jack Davie came ridin' through the woods,
Singin' so loud and merry
That the green hills all around him rang
And he charmed the heart of a lady
And he charmed the heart of a lady.

"How old are you, my pretty little miss,
How old are you, my lady?"
She answered him with a "Gee, he, he.
I'll be sixteen next summer,
I'll be sixteen next summer."

"Come go with me, my pretty little miss,
Come go with me, my lady:
I'll take you across the deep blue sea
Where you never shall want for money,
Where you never shall want for money.

"Won't you pull off those high-heeled shoes,
All made of Spanish leather?
Won't you put on some low-heeled shoes,
And we'll ride off together,
And we'll ride off together?"

She soon pulled off those high-heeled shoes,
All made of Spanish leather,

The modern folk-songs are most popular with the young people

She then put on those low-heeled shoes,
And they rode off together,
And they rode off together.

'Twas late at night when the landlord came,
Inquirin' for his lady.
He was posted by a fair young maid;
"She's gone with Black Jack Davie,
She's gone with Black Jack Davie."

"Go bridle me my noble steed,
Go saddle me my derby;
I'll ride to the east, I'll ride to the west,
Or overtake my lady,
Or overtake my lady."

He rode till he came to the deep below,
The stream was deep and muddy.
The tears came tricklin' down his cheeks;
For there he spied his lady,
For there he spied his lady.

"How can you leave your house and land,
How can you leave your baby,
How can you leave your husband dear,
To go with Black Jack Davie,
To go with Black Jack Davie?"

"Very well can I leave my house and land,
Very well can I leave my baby,
Much better can I leave my husband dear,
To go with Black Jack Davie,
To go with Black Jack Davie."

She soon run through her gay clothing
Her velvet shoes and stockings.
The gold ring off her finger was gone
And the gold plate off her bosom,
And the gold plate off her bosom.

"Oh once I had a house and land
A feather bed and money,
But now I've come to an old straw pad,
With nothing but Black Jack Davie,
With nothing but Black Jack Davie."

The hand of tradition is working to create different puzzling versions in the ballads today. Ellen Crowder of Gouges Creek was an aunt of Norma Grindstaff of Beaver Creek. Norma's mother and Ellen Crowder were children of Grandma McClellan, from whom they learned the old songs. Both Norma and Ellen sing the same songs to their children in forms akin but interestingly different. Take for example "The Hangman's Song" ("The Maid Freed From the Gallows").

Ellen Crowder sings,

Oh hangman, oh hangman, just wait a while,
Just wait a little while!
I believe I see my dear father,
He's travelled for many a mile.

Oh father, oh father, have you brought me your gold,
Or have you bought me free,
Or have you come to see me hung,
All on that lonesome tree?

Oh daughter, oh daughter, I've brought you no gold,
Nor I've not bought you free.
For I have come to see you hung
All on that lonesome tree.

And the daughter petitions in the same form each of her relatives in turn until she comes to her lover.

Oh true love, oh true love, have you brought me your gold,
Or have you bought me free,
Or have you come to see me hung,
All on that lonesome tree?

Oh sweetheart, oh sweetheart, I've brought you my gold,
And I have bought you free,

Children are watching from the porch, with a fat hound at their feet

For I've not come to see you hung,
All on that lonesome tree.

Norma Grindstaff sings it thus:

Hangman, old hangman, hold your rope,
Wait just a little while.
I think I see my father coming,
He's travelled many a mile.

Oh father, oh father, have you brought me your gold,
Or have you bought me free,
Or have you come to see me hung,
All on that lonesome tree?

Daughter, oh daughter, I've brought you no gold,
Nor I've not bought you free,
For you have stolen the golden cup,
And hangèd you must be.

And the maid petitions each of her kin in turn as in the other version, receiving each time the reply which explains the hanging (For you have stolen the golden cup). When the lover comes, the reply is different again.

> Sweetheart, oh sweetheart, I've brought you my gold,
> And I have bought you free,
> For I've not come to see you hanged,
> But married we shall be.

"The Hangman's Song" is one of the oldest, simplest, and most impersonal of the traditional ballads. Rooted in the ballad impulse of the middle ages, it has spread all over Europe. It is the Faroe Song of the Frisian pirates. There are Russian, Sicilian, and Esthonian versions and fifty Finnish variants beside the English form known as "The Maid Freed From the Gallows." It is a living vital song today throughout the whole region of the Carolina Blue Ridge.

It was the first traditional ballad I ever heard. Mrs. Blandford Burgess, who had lived in the beautiful narrow Beaver Creek Valley while Mr. Burgess was superintending the Wiseman mines, told me that Norma Grindstaff could sing the old songs and offered to take me to her. We drove up the road along Beaver Creek as far as we could, and left the car. It was possibly a two-mile walk to the Grindstaff house from there. Up the stony trail Little Yellow Mountain blocked the Valley. The foothills of Big Yellow Mountain swelling opposite hid the familiar outline of the mountain. Directly across the road beyond the creek rose the sharp escarpment of Raven's Cliff. The Grindstaff house itself snuggled cozily against a fringe of woodland on a rising knoll, L-shaped, with a porch running two sides of the angle. There are no telephones on Beaver Creek and naturally we were unexpected.

A woman washing under the trees by the side of the house, with the kettle boiling over the wash fire, paused in her work to find out what we wanted. She was a lodger with five children who lived in the house along with the Grindstaffs, who also had five children at home. Mrs. Grindstaff, who was at work in the garden, received us without visible embarrassment in spite of the lack of preparation for our coming. There were thirteen people living in five rooms and accommodating themselves to conditions amicably. If, as has been said, civilization is the art of living together, here was a simple and agreeable example.

We went up on the porch and sat down. The younger children from both families were looking over pails of strawberries together. They looked at us shyly with half averted eyes and went on with the berries. A fat fox hound slept under the grapevine at the foot of the porch. Across the road the gray and green of Raven's Cliff shimmered in the heat. Mrs. Grindstaff had been hoeing all day in the sun. She panted as she climbed the steep steps to the porch and admitted that she was "fair whipped down." It seemed an imposition to expect her to sing. At last we asked hesitatingly for a ballad, and fixing her quiet eyes on the mountain, she folded her hands and sang. The transition from speech to song was made without an effort.

I had read the words of "The Hangman's Song," but they had given me no idea of the power that has made it live. Mrs. Grindstaff attempted no expression or interpretation. It was only the age old text and the age old tune that made us see the lonely tree with the dangling rope. And then the true love came, and there was no anachronism when she remarked, at the finish of the line where he says that he will marry his sweetheart, "You see, he had his license all ready, so they could get married right then."

That afternoon was the first time I heard "The Brown Girl," which is the mountain version of "Lord Thomas and Fair Eleanor" (Annet). "Lord Thomas and Fair Eleanor" is current in England, Scotland, and Ireland. The Scotch form has been called the loveliest of all ballads. As it is sung in Mitchell County, there is more kinship to the English text dating from Charles II's time. The first stanza of the English ballad, introducing Lord Thomas, the bold forester and his love, Fair Eleanor, is missing in the Mitchell County version, which runs as follows. The text quoted is that of Ellen Crowder.

THE BROWN GIRL

"Come father, come mother, come riddle us both,
Come riddle us both as one,
And tell me whether to marry fair Ellen
Or bring me the brown girl home."

"The brown girl she has house and land,
Fair Ellender she has none.
It's my advice to you, my son,
Go bring me the brown girl home."

Norma Grindstaff can sing the old songs

He called out his merry men,
By one, by two and three.
"Go saddle me up my milk-white steed.
Fair Ellender's wedding I'll see."

He rode, he rode to fair Ellender's gate,
He rattled at the lane,
Nobody so ready, fair Ellen herself,
To rise and let him in.

"Lord Thomas, Lord Thomas, what news have you brought?
What news have you brought to me?"
"I've come to ask you to my wedding today."
"Lord Thomas, bad news to me."

She called out her merry men,
By one and two and three,
"Go saddle me up my milk-white steed.
Lord Thomas' wedding I'll see."

She dressed herself so fine in silk,
In muslin and in green,
That every town that she rode through,
They took her to be some queen.

She rode, she rode to Lord Thomas' gate,
She rattled at the lane,
Nobody so ready, Lord Thomas himself,
To rise and let her in.

He took her by the lily-white hand,
He led her into the hall,
And sat her down at the head of the table,
Amongst some quality folks.

"Lord Thomas, Lord Thomas, is this your bride?
I think she looks wonderful brown,
You might have married as fair a young lady
As ever the sun shone on."

The brown girl had a pen knife in her hand
Both long and keen and sharp,
Between the long ribs and the short
She perched it about her heart.

"Lord Thomas, Lord Thomas, are you gone blind,
Or cannot you see?
Oh, don't you see my own heart's blood
Come circling down so free?"

He took the brown girl by the hand,
He led her out of his hall.
And with a sword cut off her head
And kicked it against the wall.

He put the sword against the ground
The point against his breast,
And says, "An end to three young lovers,
God send their souls to rest.

"Go dig my grave both long and wide,
Both long and wide and deep,
And put fair Ellender in my arms
The brown girl at my feet."

In Mitchell County the best known ballads are the "Children's Song," ("The Wife of Usher's Well"), "The Hangman's Song," "The House Carpenter," and "Barbara Allen."

In the mountains one may witness the actual making of a ballad. Mr. Greer tells an incident which illustrates how a ballad can spring directly from a group of simple people and have no single author. A girl named Ella, greatly beloved in her neighborhood, was burned to death. The friends of the dead girl, watching with the body on the night before the burial, commenced making verses about her, one and another adding to the growing song. It was sung at her graveside on the same day. Then it established itself as a song in the locality under the name "Sweet Ella's Grave," other singers have added to it, and parts have been forgotten.

Sometimes a ballad has an individual author. At the time when the Allens shot up the courthouse in Hillsville, Virginia, an old man gifted at making

The mad, merry, wailing string band music tempts the outsider
to a country dance

verses was so impressed with the drama of the occasion that he made a song about it called "Claude Allen." Others felt the same interest, and the ballad was eagerly seized upon. In the spring of 1932 there was a wreck on the Carolina, Clinchfield and Ohio Railroad, caused by a collision between the afternoon passenger train and a freight running off schedule. It was already a song by fair time of the same year.

The string band music of the mountains has its apotheosis in the fiddlers' convention, just as the choir singing finds its congenial locale in the singing conventions of the country churches. It is a mountain variety show, featuring songs, string music, and clog dancing. There is a charge for admission, but the informality is so complete that the audience practically entertains itself. Anyone who wants to compete for a prize mounts to the stage and takes his turn. If he has just come in from hauling spar and has on overalls, it makes no difference. The long disjointed program lasts late as the audience warms to the fun and interrupts the contests with special request numbers. To an outsider the music all sounds much alike after the first hour, but the home folks enjoy it keenly.

An outsider will do well to learn something of the ways of Toe River before

A mountain man will hardly slave through a long spring day in order to take a vacation in the same sunshine later on

he lets the mad, merry, wailing string band music tempt him to a country dance. My own initiation was mild but added something to the sum of my experience. We had heard of a dance to be held near the Little Switzerland road and agreed to go with a party. As we drew up to park on a level spot under the trees by the road side, with the string band tinkling in the old store building below us, the lights picked out the tall figure of a man in loose overalls, shirtless, his ridged brown muscles shining, and both arms folded grotesquely on his bare stomach under the bib. I guessed that at least a quart of corn lay concealed within the bulge of blue denim, and rightly, because as soon as our lights snapped off, he came up and offered it to us for a dollar and a half. We knew it was too high, and so did he, but he took our refusal indifferently without bargaining. We might be thirstier later. He stepped back into the shadows where there was a murmur of voices.

We went into the dance. The porch was crowded and dark. Someone was selling soft drinks and cake in a corner, by the light of a lantern, but the table was too hard to reach, and it was too early, anyway. Inside, the dance floor was nearly empty, faintly lighted at each end by a kerosene lamp with reflector. Staring straight ahead, strumming evenly but always a little faster, the three boys who made up the string band lounged on chairs that were perched on the narrow counter at the far end of the room. It made no difference to them whether people danced or stood and listened. They were carried away on a tide of hypnotic, rhythmic excitement, improvising, bursting into song with the sureness of abandon. Three couples, eight couples, twelve, fourteen—the floor filled. Feet shuffled, and the frail singing thread of notes spun out upon the air in a great net, tangling, confusing, drawing everything to itself. This was not the call of languorous desire and the beat-beat of a heavy tread on soft earth. It was flame sweeping down a cold wind.

Outside, the porch was a close mass of bodies, listening in shadow to the music that swirled above them and streamed past into the moonlight. The vines along the porch poles fluttered in a breeze that had inquired into the secrets of mosses and brightly-colored leaves and the frail white flowers of the high coves.

There were little groups of men and girls by the parked cars. "Sampson"* was present that night, as usual. Our own car, tightly locked, stood under the trees in the shadow. As we approached, two ragged figures, perched like crows on the rear bumper, slipped into the dark. We should have bought the corn or watched the car. Both door handles had been wrenched off with a crow bar and the gas tank had been drained. There was no way to get in but to take off the lock, if we could not get up through the floor boards. No use. The lock had to come off. Someone in the crowd offered a flashlight. Inside the door the music stopped, and the magic went out of the night, leaving only the click of steel feeling for steel in the shadow and the sound of swearing as the lock refused to yield. The friendly country of a few minutes ago had turned alien and spiteful.

Someone tall, flat-chested, and coatless squeezed through the crowd. The banjo player. He leaned over my husband, working with the lock.

"It sure hawks us orchestra boys that this had to happen to y'all's car when you come out here for to hear us play," he said. "If you-all just let us know what it costs to fix it, we'll pay it. We don't want you to take hurt coming here."

With the friendly gesture the character of the country changed again. One can never stay of the same mind about a people so hot and cold, complex and simple, cruel and kind.

*The local name for blockade.

XIX

The Burnt Mountain Wedding

Story telling goes hand in hand with the music of the mountains as the prime entertainment of private gatherings. They say that Professor Wing, who started a mountain school and library at Ledger fifty years ago, used to hire Sol Pitman by the day to come and recite his tales. Sometimes, as with Doc Hoppas, the story teller is a singer as well, and alternates songs with long spun narratives.

Doc's house lies in the narrow wooded Brushy Creek Valley, the gap that runs from Estatoe, a cluster of houses on the Asheville Highway, to Penland, on the North Toe River at the foot of Bailey's Peak. You can drive into Doc's front yard with a car in any weather if you come by way of Estatoe, although you may have to jockey about if the road is washed in the spring. If you approach by the Penland side, you will cross the river on the railroad trestle and follow the old dinky line that runs to the Hoot Owl mines.

It is a delightful walk in the long twilight of a June evening with the laurel in pink bud and pale bloom in the shadows on either side, and the great varnished rhododendron leaves reaching out like hands, with here and there the exotic pale flower against the foliage. The branch tumbles and gurgles over the rocks beside you, crossed and re-crossed by the wobbling old rails on their rotting trestles. Here and there the ties have fallen in, and there are yawning black rectangles where the water keens and boils below in the dark. An abandoned spar car stands on the track, and if you push it up the dinky line to the high point where a by-road leads to Doc's house, you will have it ready for a return trip down the valley. The box of the car has long since disappeared, but railroad ties piled on the frame will work as well, with a fence rail for a brake stick. Only as Doc said to a timid guest debating whether to venture the ride or not, "Somebody's neck will get broke yet. Hit seems to be the proper thing to throw the brake stick away as soon as the car gets going."

It is not the trip for a timid soul. The car roars down the staggering old tracks faster and faster as the grade lends momentum, tears over the weaving trestles, and is gone again before the expected cave-in occurs. At last it flashes under the open sky at the North Toe River trestle, rattles across, slows on the level and stops.

From the dinky line a short steep road skirts the "deadening" of a new corn field and turns unexpectedly into the Hoppas yard. Spruce pine trees screen the house from the road. Tonight there is a sizeable crowd on the porch. People are perched on the railing. They sit along the angle of the house wall and on the floor in the shadows. The house looms large in the semi-darkness, two wings at right angles to each other with a porch running the length of both buildings in the angle.

Doc sits at the head of the porch in a streak of moonlight, with his wife and daughter beside him. His banjo lies carelessly across his knees as he leans back talking with a neighbor about the dry weather. He has a lean, high-nosed face—scarcely lined at fifty. Everyone is waiting for the turn of conversation that will start a story. Finally something is said about the Estatoe church.

"Doc was telling a story down at the church last night," offers Mrs. Hoppas, a matronly woman more interested in weaving and gardening than singing and carrying-on.

"Hit wa'nt right in the church," corrects Doc. "I was telling some stories to the men on the church steps and I got a good laugh. Some things on Deal Ransom, it was. You know he's got an awful lot of imagination and when he's drunk he'll tell you all sorts of things there ain't a word of truth in."

Everyone relaxes to enjoy himself. Doc is warming up now.

"This one I was telling to the men happened quite a while ago," continues

Tonight there is a sizeable crowd on the Hoppas porch

Doc. "I'd just come to the house for my dinner when Deal rides in on his horse. He was living with his wife, Doley, then, (they've separated since) and he says, 'I'm hurt bad, Doc. Shot full of buckshot'—and he was holding his hand on his breast—'so I kaint get down from my horse to open the gate on top of the hill. Come up and get me through so I can get along home.'

"I knew there wa'nt anything wrong with him and he was just imaginin' it, because he looked all right, but I wanted him to get started, so I went up to the gate and let him through and then he says, 'Come on home with me and settle Doley. She's goin' to be awful mad. I kaint go home alone and face Doley.'

" 'Tell her you're shot!' I says. 'I kaint go with you. I got to get my dinner.'

" 'She won't believe me if I do tell her,' he says. 'Hit's awful when you've got no fit home to go to. Taylor Garvey just plugged me full of buckshot and Doley'll be mad at me for drinkin' again. My breast is all shot to pieces. Just look a here!'

"And he pulled his shirt open to show me, but of course there wa'nt nothing there. After a while I got him going by himself. When he got home, his wife's sister Lockie was there in the house with Doley and he called to her and says, 'Come and get me off this mule for I'm shot bad!' and she came runnin' out to get holt of him, but Doley wouldn't let her.

" 'He's not shot,' she says. 'He's drunk. Leave him where he is.'

"And then Deal hollered, 'I'm shot in the breast by Taylor Garvey and you're goin' to lose an awful good man if you don't come and help me down.'

"But Doley wouldn't do a thing for him, nor let Lockie neither, and he kept settin' there on his mule until finally he says, 'I kaint stay here forever. You're making me have to fall off to get down.' And with that he let himself go.

"But he didn't look where he was fallin' to and he went in the daubin'-hole where they took clay out to daub the chimney. Hit was full of muddy water and there he was. Wedged in with his feet out and his head out and he couldn't stir to get free. Then he yelled harder than ever for Doley, but she went on kneading bread and wouldn't even come out to have a look at him. So there he stayed until some of the neighbors came by and hauled him out. He never would have got turned loose by himself, either."

"Wasn't Deal along when they went over the Burnt Mountain to the wedding?" asks someone, anxious to keep the ball rolling.

"No. That happened pretty near a hundred years ago. Old man Gabe Cox told me about it and he was just about fifteen or sixteen when it happened. I'll tell it like hit was me, but you'll understand.

"You see hit was Christmas Eve and we were all foolin' around and plannin' to have some fun special that night, and we aimed to get some corn. You could get it most any house you went for fifty cents a gallon. (Those days everybody made up their fruit.) And then we heard there was going to be a wedding over by Bandana, the other side of the Burnt Mountain. There wa'nt a wedding so very often in those days, so we thought we'd better go to it. The man who was telling us said it was going to be at eight o'clock. Hit was four right then so we said, 'We'll have to give up going because we kaint walk across the Burnt Mountain in deep snow and get there in time to see anything.'

"But the fellow says, 'Hector McNeal ain't gone yet and it's him that's getting married.'

"And then everybody said, 'We ought to see that. Who's marrying Hector?'

"The fellow said it was Patty Gouge, Old Bob's girl. She was getting along some. About Hector's age, or I guess she was younger. He was about fifty and a widower with children.

"So we went over to Hector's, and he was flyin' around gettin' ready to get married. We told him we was going with him, and then we thought we'd better get us a little corn to take along to warm us up. The snow was deep then. Right to your knees and we knew we'd want liquor, but we couldn't find any right off and there wa'nt much time, so we went back to Hector's without it, to go with him. We knew old Bob had lots of liquor when we'd get there. He had worlds and worlds of it and he was just stillin' all the time.

"When we got to Hector's, aye jallus, he'd done gone. He'd just lit out, but we thought we'd catch him because he was breaking trail. He could sure plow through the snow some when he was in a hurry. With just five minute start he went up the Burnt Mountain so fast we didn't catch him, and we didn't see him neither, and we thought when we got to the top and looked down we'd get sight of him, but we didn't. We climbed down as fast as we could and when we got to Gouge's, the couple was on the floor and the square was marryin' them.

"After that was over we figured Old Bob would treat us, and we were pretty dry; but right off the women commenced moving the furniture

Mountain children are interested in strangers

His affairs are not pressing

Sometimes there is no road to a cabin, and everything must be brought in on a human back

around and they set three big tables. I asked what was about to take place and they said, 'There is goin' to be a big inn-fair.'

"That suited us all right because we was hungry. Right away they brought out everything they could think of to eat that they knew how to fix in those days. And when everybody was through eating they took down the tables and I said, 'What's about to take place?'

"And they said, 'A big dance.'

"And still Old Bob hadn't offered any liquor. He was missing right then, but he came back in a minute just a battlin' around all over and staggerin', and we asked what was wrong with him. But he just went out and started walking around the house. Hit was hard goin' in the snow but he made himself a regular road—he went around so much—and every time he came to a particular corner of the house he'd yell, 'Hell's to rip and plow sandy!' as loud as he could, and go around again, and when he came to the same place, he'd yell like that, saying the same thing. After a little while of doing that, back he came in the house, sober as ever.

"He didn't say a word about a drink for us, so I thought, 'Aye jallus, I'll look around a little.' You know how they used to build the old houses. Two big rooms about eighteen by twenty with an entry room between, say twelve by eighteen. That was how Bob's house was. I went into the little entry room where he kept his house-plunder. Hit was all dark in there and first thing I saw was that some others were up to the same thing. They were feelin' around and not findin' anything, most of 'em handlin' the same barrel over and over in the dark and telling each other hit was empty. Then I run onto Sheriff John Woody (he wasn't a sheriff yet but he got to be later) and he says, 'I found a big keg over in the corner but I don't rightly know if hit's water or brandy yet.'

"Then he hit it a wallop—kerwarp—to hear how it sounded, but everybody was on to him to keep quiet and not be bringing all the house folks in on us, and he couldn't tell what was in it by the sound. So we rolled it gentle, but we couldn't tell then neither.

"Then Sheriff John says, 'Set it on end and I'll tell ye.'

"And we did and rocked it for him and it went kerswish and he says, 'Hit's water or brandy because hit's too quick for molasses.'

"Then he got us to set it up sideways on another barrel and he hit it again—kerwarp. Everybody was on to him to know why he was making so

On the green slopes below the road the tree-tops are like nodding green feathers

much noise to bring in all the house folks that was dancing and he said, 'To knock the bung out and find if it's water or brandy.'

"'Don't do it,' I says to him. 'Dig a little hole in the bung with your knife and I'll get a quill,' and I ran out of the house to where the Spanish needles grew to your waist. I found me a big one and stuck it in the hole he'd made, and it fitted airtight. We knew by then hit was brandy by the smell and John said for findin' it he ought to drink first, and we agreed.

"So he took what he wanted, pulling on the quill, and then come another and another. About then there was a big thump of somebody falling.

"'Who's down?' whispers the one at the quill, stoppin' where he was.

"'Hit's me,' says Sheriff John.

"'What's wrong with you? Y've not had much to drink,' says the one at the barrel, goin' on to finish his own.

"'Hit's the truth,' says John from the floor, all stretched out. 'But I'm on a drunken spree and I never was so drunk in my life.'

"In just a few minutes there was another thump and down went another man just like John. I came up last for my drink and thump—another man was down. But I went on and had mine.

"Right off I commenced to feel it pretty good, so I thought I'd better get clar of there where they were all lyin' around and get some air. So I went out on the porch and one of the boys was leaning up against a post, hanging on to it. And so I said to him, 'What's the matter with you?'

"And he answered back just like Dave had, 'I'm on a drunken spree and I was never so drunk in my life!'

"And with that he pitched head first out into the snow. I thought I'd better be getting in where the dancing was if everybody was like to be took down that way. So I started for the room where the party was going on. There was a step-up as you went in the door, and my feet got caught and I pitched head foremost amongst them. Old Bob came runnin' up to me and says, 'What's wrong with ye?'

"And I answers, 'I'm on a drunken spree and I never was so drunk in my life!'

"Then he asks me, 'Where did ye get it? I was aimin' to give you fellows a dram bye and bye.'

"And I up and told him how we tapped the brandy barrel in the entry room with a quill. Then he commenced to take on.

"'Aye jallus,' he says. 'Hit'll kill you all. Ye've done drunk up the gas that's

"Who's comin' up the road?"

come on that brandy, and hit's been there eleven months. There's no way for it but you'll have to march now because if you don't keep movin', you're dead.'

"So they heaved up all the men that was down and put a sober one on t' either side, with the drunk one's arms around their necks, and it was lucky there was enough to go around. Such a time getting them going you never see. Old Bob says, 'When ye get to the house corner you've got to holler to keep your voice workin'!'

"And so they went around the house and around the house, yelling on the corners just like he done earlier in the night. Pretty quick, as soon as they were able, they'd turn loose to go by themselves. Such staggering and battling around you never see, and all t'once you'd see a pair of legs sticking out of a drift and somebody would fetch a feller out and set him up and say, 'Go on. Ye've got to march!'

"Then, all at once a woman came out and started tromping around after us, and we thought she came out just to mock us. But, aye jallus, it wa'nt no time till out come some more and pretty quick they was all walking too. You see the women folks had seen the quill sticking in the brandy bung and they had some too. So we all of us went around and around until gray-day and by then we were getting sobered up and the boys were saying we'd better get us some breakfast. We wanted to be on our way over the mountain because it was Christmas morning. But the housefolks couldn't give us no breakfast because there wa'nt anybody to fix it with all the women-folks out a marchin'.

"So we lined up two and two, with the bride and groom coming last, all of us hungry, and started wading the snow back. Just as we come into the little cove on the Burnt Mounting where there was a sort of a drift under the bushes, we saw a hat lyin' on the snow. One of the boys went after it, and aye jallus, it was on Sheriff John's head, and him all covered over solid with snow. Hit seems he'd just filled himself up a little bottle extra and streaked out ahead. Then he'd set down to enjoy himself and wasn't studyin' about the snow covering him at all. So we dug him out and breshed him off and marched him home and hit was Christmas morning!"

CHAPTER

XX

Kinfolks in the Hills

John McNeal, Hector McNeal's son by his first wife, lives near the roadside on Brown's Creek in the shadow of Celo Mountain, a man ninety-three years old with rusty joints, basking in the sunshine of the narrow porch on mild winter days, his worn cane in his hand and his hat pulled down over his eyes. In the yard a gorgeous gamecock struts while his fawn-colored, long-legged wives pick among the hardy plants that turn green with the least encouragement of a warm spell. Uncle John sees more than the chickens, and the flower plants circled in whitewashed automobile tires laid flat on the ground, and the chunks of wood piled generously against the outhouse and overflowing the lane.

He is watching the troops of mounted infantry of Thomas' army file under the trees, row on row, hundreds of prancing horses and blue-coated men, the proudest show he ever saw, sweeping up the Blue Ridge to Blowing Rock and down again to open the prison doors in Salisbury. The War is all smoke and marches and nameless skirmishes to Uncle John, and one clear picture— the gallant advance up the Blue Ridge.

He fought first for the Confederacy, swept in on the first enthusiastic tide, although he voted for North Carolina to stay in the Union. That was a day to

John McNeal sits basking in the sunshine on mild winter days, his worn cane in his hand and his hat pulled down over his eyes

remember, the only time he ever got drunk at a public gathering. Later he joined the Federal Army. He couldn't quiet his preference for the Union.

His mind drifts without effort through old bright landscapes. He sees his sheep and milk-cattle trot-trotting down the old Laurel turnpike to market in the dazzling sun of an early spring morning, and young and rugged as in the old days, he walks behind them, swinging a stout, laurel bough and fingering the toll pennies in his pocket.

Young John is climbing up the knoll behind his cabin with a basket of corn for the sow that beds in a hollow log under the ivy. As he ducks under the branches she squeals in terror. It cannot be from surprise at his coming. She knows him. He runs to the log and meets the snarling face of a bear, upper lip lifted, surprised in the act of tearing juicy meat from the sow he has maimed but not yet killed. The malevolent face of the beast has been sneaking up to peer at Uncle John at unexpected times for seventy years, growing bigger and meaner. The young man's gun will not fire. Wet powder. He backs off and picks at it desperately with a twig. No matter. The bear whirls clumsily and blunders away into the bushes.

Young John is trying to bed himself down comfortably by a tiny camp fire in a cove under Cat Tail Peak. A dead rattlesnake lies by a tree stump five yards away where he tossed it when he killed it a few minutes ago. He drops to the ground, springs to his feet at the crackle of a twig, and throws himself down again. The mate of the snake he killed will come, but he is half-dead for sleep. He tries to think clearly in the borderland of slumber, hanging on to sober woods sense. Then he rises, picks up chips of bark and laurel twigs until he has a pile waist high. These he distributes in a circle, being careful that there is no gap. Then he lights the wood with a brand from the fire. The dry laurel makes a crackling golden ring about him. He should have made his circle larger. When the heat grows unbearable, he stamps out the camp fire. The slowly burning bark is taking the place of the crackling laurel, and the heat moderates. The other rattler will not come upon him now when he is off his guard. He throws himself upon the ground and sleeps.

Every now and then faces and voices that cloud the old time drag Uncle John back to the present. Sons of his brothers and sisters and their children. Here is Will McNeal, his brother Arch's son, come to visit him, and Arch's grandson. Arch is long gone. He built himself a cabin backed up to the same chimney where Frankie Silvers burned her husband. Frankie's old cabin was gone, but the chimney with the fireplace stood strong as ever and saved

At the back of the Bailey homestead Miss Amanda's dahlias and larkspur struggle with the waist-high timothy

building another. Arch's wife found one of Charlie Silvers' shoeheel irons jammed into the stones of the fireplace, but she never could bear to touch it, and there it stayed to remind her every time she put a pan over the fire of the man who had been burned on those very stones.

It is not a long journey back to the beginnings of the settlement of western North Carolina, if one starts from Uncle John's birth. His father, Hector, was the son of Neal McNeal, who came to this country from Scotland in 1760 when the new world was his who had an axe and a strong right arm. Life in the mountains is all tangled into tantalizing patterns, if they could only be figured out. The relationships weave and interlace underground like tree roots. Englishes, Baileys, Penlands, Buchanans, McNeals, Wilsons, Gouges, Burlesons, Silvers, Ellises, Coxes. One of Isaac English's daughters married James Bailey's oldest son. James Bailey's wife, who was Polly Cox, was kin to John McNeal's mother (Hector McNeal's first wife). Arch McNeal married the murdered Charles Silvers' brother's widow. Doc Hoppas' wife was a Silvers.

Granny Silvers lies there in a tall post-and-spindle bed

Over in the Deyton Bend, in a white house behind tall boxwoods, lives Granny Silvers, now ninety-four, who was Roxanna Wilson and then Garrett Gouge's wife before she married David Silvers. The big, low-ceilinged room, with its brown weathered beams, cherry corner cupboard, and chest of drawers, is the very room where the wedding of Patty Gouge and Hector McNeal took place. Granny Silvers lies there today in a tall post-and-spindle bed, resting quietly under the "smoothin'-iron quilt" that she pieced so long ago, and listening to the measured tick of the square box clock. She remembers the gathering as clearly as though it were only yesterday that little Patty stood up with Hector. On the hill above the dam at Penland the Deer Park homestead retreats darkly among the trees. Pinckney and Miss Amanda, a son and daughter of James Bailey, the builder of the house, were the last to live there. When Pinckney died, Miss Amanda came to town to live, and the key was turned on the old house and its furnishings that wait for the family's return.

A path leads steeply through the rhododendron from the footbridge over the river, looking back on itself as it climbs, runs into a part of the old road, mossy and grass grown, and wanders leisurely along the boundary of the old Deer Park. Much of the tall fence still remains, the posts almost hidden by a riotous growth of poison oak. Under the trees the ground is covered with galax, strawberries, and rattleweed. A row of spruce pines screens the front face of the building, and Captain Bill vine overruns the fence. Rhododendron crowds the front corner, and the lawn is tangled with Wandering Jew. The boxwoods that came from Clear Creek in 1880 have grown to the second story, completely shading the windows toward the northeast.

Across the front the house has a double porch, partly enclosed, with a broad balustraded stairway leading from the lower porch to the upper one. There is a narrow stoop on either side of the dining room wing, one mantled by a giant wisteria, the other by a trumpet vine that climbs to the roof and then cascades back in crimson streamers. At the back of the building Miss Amanda's dahlias and larkspur struggle with the waist high timothy. A clump of tiger lilies thrusts boldly through the gate, and the once carefully tended orange tree is overwhelmed by a sprawling wisteria and a crimson rambler. Everywhere there is a riot of blossoms, and the air is sweet with their fragrance and the cool perfume of pine and herb.

The austere loneliness of the place greets you solemnly on the iron door stone. Entering the house from the long porch you expect the smell of hymn

For a number of years Pinckney Bailey made most of the entries
in the family book

She has time now to sit down and rest

books and church carpets. The hall within is papered with the intricate light and dark geometric figures of the '80's. In the deep twilight of the room to the left, beyond the panelled door, the bulk of a corner cupboard is scarcely discernible. A candle stand and a low rocker edge up to the bare hearth. From the opposite wall a cherry chest of drawers faces the porch door. On either side of the hall door stand cherry four-posters, made up for the night with valance and gray-white spread and mountainous feather beds. All the intimate things of daily living lie about as though left only yesterday. A partly emptied medicine bottle on the mantel, a calendar dated 1906 on the wall, and drawn up to the bedside, where Miss Amanda could sit down to take off her shoes, a low chair with dainty spindled back. Beyond in the dining room at the end of the hall the chairs are gone, but the tables stand, end to end, ready for the cloth. A few odd dishes line the walnut corner cupboard, and the old cooking vessels hang in the cool pantry. A box clock, silent and dusty, stands on the poplar mantel that James Bailey joined so neatly for his new home long ago.

There are four fireplaces downstairs and two more upstairs, with rusty fire dogs and a light powder of ashes. On the second floor the four-posters and spool-turned cottage steads in the four generous chambers stand ready with quilts, woven coverlets, and fat pillows, among a confusion of old chests, neatly dove-tailed stands and tables, ornate curled mica medallions, and faded photographs of bearded men.

The bedroom above the kitchen, overlooking the flower garden, is crowded with the shiny, yellow oak of the '90's. There, upon a nail by a flat-topped desk, hangs the family record book, with its informal jottings of first snows, mowings, and plantings, mingled with births, marriages, and deaths.

1858　First cane in the mountains.
1876　Big Barn built. Covered five times.
1886　Earthquake August 31, 9:15 o'clock.
1898　Old Nell killed. August.
1901　May 21, Big flood. May 28–29, Roan Mountain covered with
　　　　snow.
　　　Sept. 6, McKinley shot.
　　　September 15, McKinley died.
1902　June 24th, Acorns blasted.
　　　September 14, First frost.

Mrs. Dixon was a tall mountain woman, crippled with rheumatism,
but a fine cook and housekeeper

December 25, Blowing snow. Oh, how cold!

December 27, River frozen over. Walking on ice.

1903   April 29, Train came to Conley's Camp.

Oct. 3, Snowbirds seen in the garden Saturday morning.

1906   June 21, Big hail storm.

After 1906, the entries became fewer as life narrowed and quieted at the homestead. Pinck and Amanda were growing old.

1918   Jan. 24, Wesley married Lucy Davidson of Statesville.

1924   April 2, John died. Bn. '48.

And then a new handwriting appears with the brief entry

1928   Jan. 26, Pinckney Bailey died.

For a number of years Pinckney Bailey had made most of the entries in the family book. After his death the records were continued as before. Where one hand laid down the pen, another took it up. The pages in that account book reflect the flowing continuity of all Toe River life. Where does today begin in the hills, when yesterday has not yet left off?